101 Quick & Easy Woodworking Projects

Charles R. Self

Sterling Publishing Co., Inc. New York

Dedication

To Frances, for letting me work my way through this one.

Library of Congress Cataloging-in-Publication Data

Self, Charles R.
    101 quick & easy woodworking projects / by Charles R. Self.
      p. cm.
    Includes index.
    ISBN 0-8069-8298-5
    1. Woodwork. I. Title. II. Title: 101 quick and easy
woodworking projects. III. Title: One hundred one quick & easy
woodworking projects. IV. Title: One hundred and one quick &
easy woodworking projects.
    TT180.S397 1992
    684'.08—dc20   92-25310
                                          CIP

Edited by R. P. Neumann

10 9 8 7 6 5 4 3 2 1

Published in 1992 by Sterling Publishing Company, Inc.
387 Park Avenue South, New York, N.Y. 10016
© 1992 by Charles R. Self
Distributed in Canada by Sterling Publishing
% Canadian Manda Group, P.O. Box 920, Station U
Toronto, Ontario, Canada M8Z 5P9
Distributed in Great Britain and Europe by Cassell PLC
Villiers House, 41/47 Strand, London WC2N 5JE, England
Distributed in Australia by Capricorn Link Ltd.
P.O. Box 665, Lane Cove, NSW 2066
Manufactured in the United States of America
All rights reserved

Sterling ISBN 0-8069-8298-5

Contents

6 Plywood Projects 94

7 Projects Just for Kids 123

Appendix 155

Metric Conversion 158

Index 159

Acknowledgments

I received a lot of necessary help from a lot of people and many companies in the process of putting this book together. My friend Bobby Weaver always stood ready to help, and you'll see his hands in many shots. Photographing someone else's hands is always easier than photographing my own; Bobby helps further by having a pair of very skillful hands.

I received tools, materials information and assistance from AMT, Black & Decker, Dremel, Makita, Porter-Cable, Ryobi, Skil, American Clamping Corporation, Adjustable Clamp Company, Stanley Tools and Stanley Hardware, CooperTools, United Gilsonite Labs (finishes), Franklin Chemical Industries International (adhesives), the Southern Forest Products Association, Hickson International (Wolmanized Wood), Norton (sandpapers), Campbell-Hausfeld air compressors, DeVilbiss (air compressors), Ingersoll Rand (air compressors), Georgia-Pacific (for letting me use again some projects I once did for them), the California Redwood Association, the American Plywood Association, and Louisiana-Pacific. And there may be others I've overlooked; if so, let me apologize in advance.

Introduction

The projects in this book are reasonably "quick & easy." There may be some room for argument, because a few will take some time, upwards of a weekend, and require more than one person to assemble. And a project that may require two people may be a great deal easier and safer with three people.

I've designed a few projects that took less than an hour from the start of my pencil on paper to a finished product—not including time for glue drying, and finishing. Finishing is a process that requires a lot of care even for simple work, with more complex clear finishes needing truly lots of work. Some people wish to spend the time, while others don't. For instance a project, such as a large wall mirror frame, of solid cherry that can be assembled, glued, and clamped in an afternoon may need quite a bit more time to finish. The project will get about five or six coats of satin-finish tung oil, requiring at least three days' time, and a couple extra hours of sanding and smoothing with steel wool.

The same project may be made of pine, stained and quickly coated with a spray or brush-on polyurethane, in two coats, with minimal sanding between coats. The finish time is reduced to a single day, most of which is spent waiting for the first coat to dry. The project might also be made of even cheaper pine, sanded, and painted. Finish time is reduced to an hour or so, with almost no effort needed. The finish time on a single project can vary from one to thirty-six hours (plus drying time of the coat in each case).

So to call these projects "Quick & Easy" means that the tasks of cutting, preparing, and assembling may be reasonably swift and uncomplicated; but the finishing time depends on several choices you are responsible for and may add up to a lot more than making the actual project.

Charles R. Self
Bedford, Virginia

1 · Guide to Tools with Accessories Projects

Many of the projects presented here and in following chapters can be readily made with portable power tools, as well as hand tools. Some can be made more quickly with stationary power tools, and with accessories that you can make. No matter what tool you use—but especially with power tools—use safety devices, such as saw guards, wear appropriate clothing, and wear safety glasses or a face shield of some kind.

Handtools

Handtools needed for woodworking include the claw hammer, handsaw, screwdrivers of various types, planes, chisels, mitre box, nail sets, measuring tapes and rules, squares, levels, a brace and bit set.

Scribe and combination square make a good measurement-transferring pair.

Measuring Tools

Measuring tapes come in many lengths and widths. For most project purposes, lengths above a dozen feet aren't needed. Folding rules come in 6′ and 8′ lengths. Flat rules are available in metal and wood.

The basics of measuring include adding a tilt to the tape or rule when a mark is made. Marks may be made with standard pencils, carpenter's pencils or scribes.

Squares

Squares for woodworking include the try square, the combination square, the speed square, and the framing square. Squares of two types are essential. The basic, or try, square is a rigid form of metal, or wood and metal. The blade size will be 8″ to 12″ long, in inch or metric markings.

Try squares also serve as setup tools.

Combination squares have blades that slide in the handles, offering 90- and 45-degree markings, with slightly less accuracy than a try square.

Framing, carpenter's, and roofing squares are versions of a stamped metal L with a 2″ wide blade and a 1½″ wide tongue.

Handsaws

Saws are the primary cutting tools for woodworking. For our projects a 10-point panel saw; a 12″ or larger backsaw; a coping, or scroll, saw will do. For metal, or harder plastics, get a hacksaw. For rougher cuts, one of the newer hard-tooth saws, with eight points per inch, works well. A mitre box is also handy.

Stanley's Short Cut saw.

Hammers

Hammers are available in many styles and sizes, but for our 101 projects, a good-quality 16-ounce, curved claw is suitable. (Head weights vary from 13 ounces to 28 ounces.) I prefer a fibreglass handle to all others, but often use tubular metal, and wood. For the A-frame swing set in Chapter 2 (Project 5), we used a framing hammer on the larger (16d) nails.

Deckmaster hammer.

Screwdrivers

Screwdrivers come in all the obvious head styles, to fit old and new head patterns. Select for head style, and for quality. As a basic recommendation, it is wise to go with a reasonable-length shank, say 6″ to 8″, as these are the easiest to control.

Staplers

Staplers are useful for attaching fabrics, and light woods to heavier woods. There are air-powered staples as well as hand and electric staplers. Air-powered staplers are simpler, and seem more efficient and less likely to jam than electric versions.

Electric Drills

Standard electric drills come in many versions and chuck sizes. Select for durability as well as power. Drills are one tool where buying cheap can't pay. For most purposes, a ⅜″ chuck drill, with a variable speed, reversible motor drawing 3.5 or more amperes works well.

For driving screws, use a clutched drill. Any variable-speed drill does a fair job of driving screws, but a clutched variable-speed drill stops driving before it torques the head off.

Cordless electric drills are worth considering, even as replacements for corded drills. These drills offer the same features you find in corded drills, with slightly lower capacities in wood, steel, and masonry. If you go cordless, get a drill with a battery pack that charges quickly, in less than three hours, and buy a second battery pack.

Skil's Top Gun 12-volt cordless drill is a variable-speed reversible model, with two speed ranges.

General's 350-1 table saw with sliding table offers impressive power, and a 48" crosscut capacity in front of the blade (11" is pretty much on the high end of standard without a sliding table).

The smaller, lighter Makita also has a sliding table, but exchanges capacity for portability.

Bayonet saws often partly take the place of band and scroll saws.

Power Saws

Selecting a table saw is a moderately simple job even with the wide variety on the market. Blade size may range from 4" up to 14", while power can vary from fractional to three-phase multi-horsepower. Tight tolerances, tables precisely machined, and well-made adjusters are needed. Mitre slots must be precise, and the rip fence sturdy and accurate. Both mitre gauge and rip fence can be replaced with aftermarket types, but such units are expensive. Several portable saws offer surprising accuracy.

The band saw does almost everything the table saw does, with no danger of kickback (the prime drawback of table saws, and a function of blade design and rotation that can't be totally eliminated). The band saw also offers great ease on jobs the table saw cannot do at all well (cutting curves).

A related tool is the hand-held jigsaw or sabre saw. These power saws are also excellent for cutting curves and especially holes, which the band saw cannot do.

Circular Saw

Circular saws offer more speed than jigsaws, and can be more accurate. Blade diameters range from 4" to 16".

A circular saw needs a thick base plate that is easy to adjust for depth; an 8' to 10' long cord; a top handle for easier control; a 7¼" blade size; and at least a 10-ampere motor.

Circular saws are used in construction work and woodworking to form mitre and butt joints. Their accuracy depends on both your experience and the jigs used to assist in the cut.

A carbide-tipped blade is usually best. The blade may be a combination for general use—able to do rip

Circular saws may be as small as this, Porter-Cable's Trim Saw.

Black & Decker's 7¼″ is the size that is close to an industry standard.

and crosscuts. For the best mitres, use a planer combination blade.

The rip guide helps make excellent long rips. It adjusts to allow the appropriate cutoff of material with the grain, but is not used for cross-grain cuts. Easily used, the guide shaft slips into slots on the saw base, and a screw is tightened when the distance is set. Guide on the outside edge of the work to make the cut. For deeper rip cuts, and for crosscuts, a guide board is needed.

Skil's "Edge" blade offers fast cuts with a thin kerf.

1 ◆ Making Your Own Guide Board

Go to a lumberyard and have them cut you a piece of tempered hardboard (¼″ thick) about a foot wide and 5′ to 10′ long (you may wish to make several of these guides in different lengths).

Materials
- 8′ × ¼″ × 12″ tempered hardboard
- 8′ × ⅜″ × 3″ fir
- twelve ½″ × No. 6 flathead wood screws
- Wood glue

Tools
- 12–18 C-clamps
- Screwdriver
- Drill and ¹⁄₁₆″ bit for pilot holes
- Small countersink

To the tempered hardboard, glue and screw a ⅜″ thick × 3″ wide straight board. Fasten along the long side, flush with one long edge of the tempered hardboard.

The last step in preparing the jig is to set it in place. After measuring the width of the saw base plate to the blade, clamp the jig to the material being cut. Cut both jig and material. Afterwards, measure the material, and place the jig so the cutoff edge is at the edge of the cut: you must always use the same circular saw with this jig (mark both jig and saw for use together, if you have more than one circular saw).

Give thought to a power mitre or compound mitre saw, or portable radial-arm saw as a supplement to other saws, an aid in compound cutting chores, and accuracy in mitring.

Routers

Routers are very useful tools; if you expect to keep on woodworking, get one. Select a model with at least one horsepower, preferably with a ½″ collet, though a ¼″ collet will do. The smaller collet chuck diameter makes for less accurate machining, but less costly bits. A plunge router is handy, but is not essential.

Dremel's little router table is great for small work.

This 1½ HP Porter-Cable is a workhorse general-duty router. The D handle is, I feel, better for control in some uses. Basic motor comes as a straight knob handle and a plunge model as well.

Router Tables

Router tables may be bought or built.

Some of the same bits that are useful on a router table may also be used, with great care, freehand, but others are not suitable for freehand use. Freud's box-joint bit is a case in point. It requires a powerful router to work well, and has a strong tendency to throw the work, or jerk the router around. It is far safer to mount the router in a table.

Other router bits may be used freehand, but do a smoother job on a router table. All safety rules, regardless of bit used, must be observed.

2 ♦ Router Table Construction

Materials
- ¾″ × 36″ × 24″ birch plywood (or fir)
- ¾″ × 36″ × 24″ fir plywood
- four 29″ two-by-four
- two 22″ four-by-four
- two 20″ four-by-four (cut down to a full 2″ thick)
- two 27″ two-by-four (cross-members)
- two 16″ two-by-four (side horizontal members)
- 36″ × 24″ laminate for top (if desired)
- 8″ × 12″ Lexan or ¼″ aluminum plate for router base and holder
- ¼″ dowel stock
- ⅜″ dowel stock
- wood glue
- contact cement

Tools
- router and ½″ chamfer bit
- laminate edging bit
- mitre box
- ¾″ chisel
- square
- measuring tape
- drill, ¾″ brad point, or Forstner, drill bit
- mallet
- plane or jointer
- twelve small bar clamps, or C-clamps
- four 36″ bar clamps
- pad sander and 100-grit sandpaper

Begin by checking measurements, planing two-by-four stock down to 3″ from 3½″, using the jointer or a hand plane.

Laminate the top pieces using wood glue, and set aside to dry for at least three hours. Clamp every 8″.

Cut legs and cross-members to length, and then cut four-by-four stock to size, and measure for mortises. Cut tenons from two-by-four stock, as shown on the drawings, and cut matching mortises in the thicker stock.

Width measurements for tenons on the horizontal side members are not shown on the drawings, but should be ⅝″, centered in the upright. The front and rear horizontal members are dowelled from the outsides of the legs, after being clamped, with glue, in place. Dowels go all the way in from the leg exteriors, and are well glued. If you wish, use a contrasting color of wood for the dowels.

Once mortises are cut, assemble the leg unit, dry at first, then with glue and clamps. All mortise-and-tenon work may be replaced with long dowels drilled straight through, or with biscuit joinery.

Place the top, centered, on the leg assembly. You may assemble with lag screws run up through the top members. If this is desired, prepare pilot holes by drilling 1½″ deep, 1½″ diameter holes with a Forstner bit, and then come up through that with a ¼″ brad point bit until the bit touches the bottom of the top. Use a ⅛″ bit to finish the pilot hole drilling. Insert a 2″ lag screw in each hole (use two holes per support member), and draw the top down tight.

Alternatively, you may wish to use dowels to fasten the plywood top to the cross-members. If so, position the top on the cross-members, and mark the middle of the cross-member positions on the surface of the top. Next,

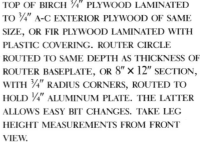

TOP OF BIRCH ¾″ PLYWOOD LAMINATED TO ¾″ A-C EXTERIOR PLYWOOD OF SAME SIZE, OR FIR PLYWOOD LAMINATED WITH PLASTIC COVERING. ROUTER CIRCLE ROUTED TO SAME DEPTH AS THICKNESS OF ROUTER BASEPLATE, OR 8″ × 12″ SECTION, WITH ¾″ RADIUS CORNERS, ROUTED TO HOLD ¼″ ALUMINUM PLATE. THE LATTER ALLOWS EASY BIT CHANGES. TAKE LEG HEIGHT MEASUREMENTS FROM FRONT VIEW.

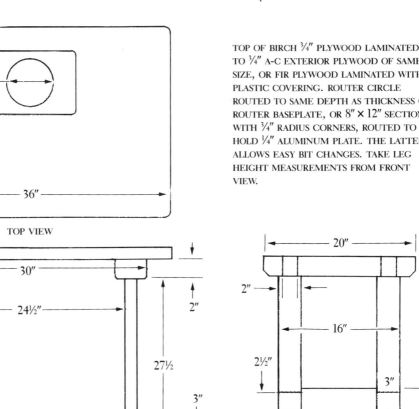

TOP VIEW

FRONT VIEW

2-1. *Router table plan.*

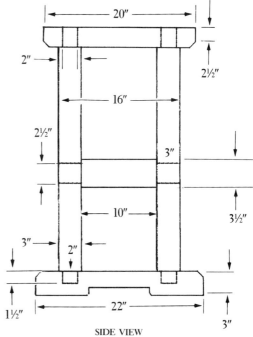

SIDE VIEW

11

clamp in place, making sure nothing moves. Use a ⅜″ brad point drill bit to drill into the cross-members, with a total hole of depth 2⅛″, to accept the 2″ dowels. You may use a contrasting-color dowel if you're using a birch top, or you may simply smooth down the top of a standard dowel before using contact cement to add a Micarta laminate cover to the top surface.

The top is cut to accept the 8″ × 12″ router plate, with a ¼″ × ⅜″ rabbet around the edges to let the plate sit level with the top surface. You may install adjuster screws in the edges of the plate, if you desire, but they shouldn't be needed, if you've routed the ledge with precision. Do that in three passes to prevent chipping.

Top corners may be rounded on a 1″ radius, and, before that's done, you may wish to rout a groove to fit one of your mitre gauges; use an edge guide to rout the groove, and use great care.

At one point, I designed a fence for this table, but now find that quite a few fence assemblies offer better accuracy and more options than my home-built fence.

---

3 ◆ Router Jig

Dadoes and grooves are quickly and readily cut with routers. Setup is often faster than with a table saw. All sorts of jigs are possible to make sure the spacing is proper, but the simplest one is a set of spaced bars inside which the router moves. The space between bars needs to equal the width of your router base.

Materials
- **one-by-three or one-by-four stock, cut to length**
- **wood screws**
- **wood glue**

Tools
- **square**
- **measuring tape**
- **saw**
- **screwdriver**

Underneath side guide bars are end bars to equal the width of the router base, plus the width of the guide bars. Use straight one-by-three or one-by-four stock for all pieces. Make sure the corners are square. Assemble with screws and glue for long-term use.

Butt the jig on the side of the board to be dadoed. Clamp lightly at the end away from where you'll start cutting. The first cut makes a groove in the jig's end spacer; mark the middle of the groove. That mark serves as the line-up point for succeeding dadoes. Set the depth carefully. Start the router and run it across the workpiece.

Guide bars must be longer than the stock being cut. Because a particular project calls for routing a single 12″ wide piece, don't figure that will be the widest you'll ever cut. It is often easier to match pieces—for bookcase sides and other projects—if all of the cuts are made on all pieces at the same time. Making the bars at least 3′ long is a good idea. With the line-up point marked, you can make dadoes of any width: generally, single-pass dadoes done with a router are best limited to about 1¼″, using a mortising bit.

Biscuit Joiners

Biscuit joiners, also known as plate joiners, are circular blade tools that cut a kerf 0.156″ thick, with a loose fit for flat, football-shaped biscuits that are 0.148″ thick. Biscuits come in three widths, No. 0, No. 10, No. 20. Plates absorb water from the glue and swell past 0.160″.

Biscuit joiner and biscuits.

Accuracy is easier to attain with biscuits than with dowels. The slot cut to accept the plate allows adjustment along the length of the biscuit, while a dowel pegs you to a point and keeps you there. If you've drilled your dowel holes a fraction of an inch off, your project must be a fraction of an inch off. With plates, you'll never be much more than a small fraction off because of the way the machines are made. Any miss, and you slip things around until the mate is perfect.

With biscuits, do not open any packages until you need the biscuits, and reseal as soon as possible. Store the packages in a dry area.

The biscuits are of solid beech—stamped to size after being sawn into laths.

Other Useful Tools

There are a variety of additional tools that may come in handy; I'll mention a few. Planers can save much money in lumber as you find yourself doing a lot of woodworking. Drill presses increase precision, and the good ones are quite versatile. Whenever you are drilling or using your drill press, match the cutting tool to the job. And whenever countersinking is called for, a quality countersink will help give neat work.

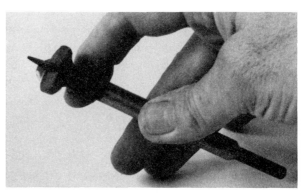

Stanley's Powerbore bit is a fairly low-cost tool that provides very neat hole cutting.

Planers save much money in lumber when you do a lot of woodworking. This is Makita's 12".

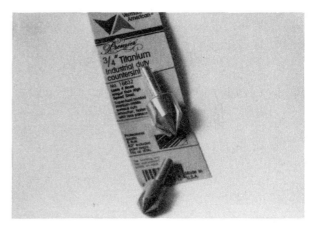

Quality countersinks help give neat work.

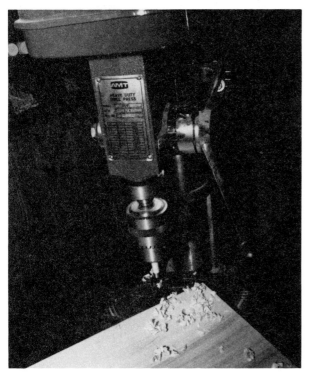

Drill presses increase precision, and good ones are versatile.

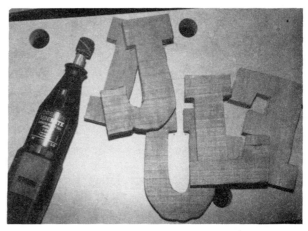

Mini-Mite cordless is great for cleanup on small jobs.

Any finishing sander will do, but you may want to have a variety of sanding tools. Small belt and disc sanders are exceptionally helpful with smaller projects. A small rotary tool with a sanding attachment can help with cleanup on small jobs and hard-to-get places.

Small belt and disc sanders like this Dremel are exceptionally helpful with smaller projects.

One indispensable tool, of which you should have several varieties, is a woodworking clamp. Woodworking clamps fall into four basic categories; bar clamps, C-clamps, band clamps, and hand screws. The largest number of types fall into the bar clamp category. Hand screws work well to clamp nonparallel surfaces, and do not creep. From time to time, other clamps such as spring clamps are of help.

Heavy-duty Bessey K body bar clamp.

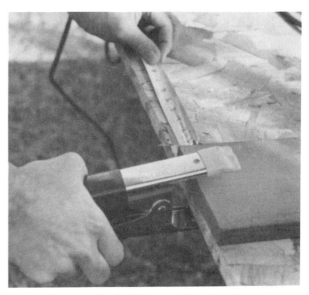

Spring clamp used to hold saw-guiding board in place.

4 ♦ Workbench

One of the most important tools for the woodworker, or any hobbyist working with tools, is a good workbench. Consider buying one or making your own. Two workbench projects are presented; this one and another in the chapter of plywood projects (Chapter 6). The plywood workbench is simple to construct, but is perhaps more of an auxiliary table for light-duty work. This unit is stable and sturdy, and has easily accessible tool storage on pegboard and rack, plus bench stops.

Materials
- two ¾" × 4' × 8' A-C sanded plywood, interior
- ¼" × 4' × 8' pegboard
- four × four × 12' (legs)
- two 10' × 2" × 4" (front and back stretchers; back supports)
- two 10' × 1" × 4" (side stretchers)
- 1" × 12" × 3' (tool rack base)
- four 1" × 3" × 12' (tool rack frame; tool shelf)
- ¾" × ¾" × 6' (bottom shelf cleat)
- 28' ¾ round (shelf moulding)
- 12' × ¼" × 1¾" lattice (banding for bench top)
- 1¼" brads
- No. 8 × ¾", 1¼", 1½" flathead Phillips screws
- No. 10 × 1½", 3", 2" flathead Phillips screws
- 5⁄16" × 4½", 5", 2" carriage bolts, nuts, washers
- eight 3" corner braces with screws
- four 3" flat L-braces
- 16d finishing nails

Tools

- tape measure
- try square
- framing square
- mallet
- claw hammer
- circular saw
- drill, clutched, with Phillips driver bit, and ⅜", ½", ¾", 1" drill bits
- adjustable wrench
- handsaw
- backsaw
- coping saw
- block plane
- 1" chisel
- ¾" chisel
- four 3" C-clamps
- four short bar clamps
- utility knife
- nail set
- wood glue
- 100-grit sandpaper
- finishing sander

4-1.   Workbench. (Courtesy of Stanley Tools.)

Begin by laying out the four-by-four legs for height, and all other cuts. Work the legs in mirrored pairs (one pair for the left, one for the right); each leg needs to be marked for position before anything other than length is determined. Up 5½" from leg bottom, mark and cut a dado to take the lower stretcher; layout marks are 5½" and 9". Depth is ¾". The leg tops are rabbeted to take the top stretchers, with the rabbet going 3½" down from the top, ¾" deep. Note the meetings of the dadoes and of the rabbets to allow assembly of two stretcher ends on each leg.

When making the cuts, use a backsaw to cut inside the marked lines, exactly to the depth line (not into it). Cut several times after making the outside cuts and chisel out waste.

Mark, square, and cut four 25" pieces of one-by-four for side stretchers. Mark in 2½" from each end on two pieces, and mark points at ¾" and 2¾" on the marked line. These are the top side stretchers. On the other two pieces, mark in 1⅜" from each end line, and mark at ¾" and 2¾" for screw holes in the bottom side stretchers.

Drill for 2" screws, and assemble the leg sets.

Cut four two-by-four front and back stretchers to 58½" lengths. Stand the two leg sets up, and clamp a top stretcher in position, using a bar clamp on both ends. Measure 2½" from each end, including the side stretchers, draw a line, and then mark that line at 1" and 2½".

Use a ⅜" bit at each point, drilling through the stretcher and the leg. Fasten with 4½" carriage bolts, nuts, and washers. Tighten tightly. Do the same for the bottom stretcher. Repeat for both stretchers on the other side.

Add the ¾" square cleat (bottom shelf support) to the inside of each bottom stretcher. Cut two pieces 16½" long, and drill for 1¼" No. 8 screws. Locate the first screw 3" from one end, the others at 3" intervals. Do the same for the other cleat. Glue and screw flush with top of stretcher.

The frame is ready, so it's time to make the shelf. Rip 18" × 96" from each of the two sheets of ¾" A-C plywood. Crosscut one to 58½". All plywood cuts are best made with a circular saw and saw guide, with the good face down. Install the shelf, dropping it onto the stretchers, and making sure it's positioned correctly. There will be ¾" showing all around. Drill pilot holes and countersinks for 1¼" screws on all sides, 6" on center. Trim with the ¾ round moulding, cut to fit. Glue and nail the moulding with 1¼" brads.

Cut and fit the top. For strength and stability, a double thickness of plywood is used. Cut both remaining pieces of plywood (after the 18" pieces were cut off) to 71½". You may either glue up the top or clamp together securely, good side *down*, drilling on 6" centers around the perimeter, and assembling using 1¼" No. 8 flathead screws. The screw assembly means the top may be easily replaced when it wears badly. The glue assembly is a bit

15

stiffer, and readily allows for a hardboard or other covering when wear shows up badly.

Cut bench stop slots, if any. A row or two of holes and two hold-down clamps will do a good many bench stop jobs as well.

To secure top to leg frame, set top in place, good side up, with a 10″ overhang on the left end. Measuring from the back, mark points at 11¼″ and 21½″. These points mark the back edges of bench stop slots. Cut two stops from a 1 × 4, making each 7″ long. Set a stop in place at each of the marks and use a utility knife or scribe to mark around the stop. Use a ¾″ bit to drill four holes inside each rectangle. Test the fit of the stops.

Cut bolt slots in the stops. Locate and mark the centerline, and mark 3″ and 4½″ from one end. Use a ⅜″ bit to drill holes within that rectangle. Fit the 5/16″ carriage bolts in their slots and place the stops in their slots.

The parts as now assembled are heavy, and require at least two adults to lift and move. Place top, good side down, on sawhorses. Set the completed frame upside down, atop the work surface. Stops project up through left side of the bench top. Align the frame flush with the back edge of top, and slide until the left legs are against the stops.

Use eight 3″ corner braces and their screws to attach the frame to the bench top. Place three braces along side of front stretcher, three inside the back stretcher, and one inside each end.

The bench is now set on its own feet. Drill left top stretcher for stop bolts. Set stops flush with bench. Mark

hole locations through stops at the tops of the slots. Drill holes with the ⅜″ bit. Use a 5″ carriage bolt for the front stop and a 2″ bolt with the back. Insert bolts from inside stretcher, add washers, and screw on wing nuts.

Measure, cut, and fit 1¾″ wide lattice trim to the bench end. Attach end pieces first, after shaving down to 1½″ with a block plane. Measure front to overlap ends, and glue and nail in place with 1¼″ brads every 6″. Front strip is planed flush with the top.

Make the pegboard back. Lay four pieces, cut to 72″ (two) and 28″ (two), out and assemble with flat corner braces. Side pieces must butt inside the top and bottom pieces. Cut pegboard to 72″ × 33″, and cut two 42¾″ pieces of one-by-three and one 67″ piece for the front frame.

Lay one 42¾″ piece on each end of the new workbench, and place the 67″ piece between them. Assemble each corner with the 3½″ (16d) finishing nail. Lay the pegboard on top, squaring it flush with the top corner joints. Lay the back frame assembly squarely on top of the pegboard. The two 42¾″ pieces stick down a good distance here.

Check flush fit on all sides and corners and clamp on two sides. Drill 6″ on center, drilling from the back, through the frame, pegboard, and into the front frame. Fasten using 1½″ × No. 8 flathead screws. Fasten through bottom of pegboard into back frame using ¾″ × No. 8 screws.

The backboard tool rack is a simple unit. Crosscut one-by-twelve pine to 72″. Crosscut one-by-three pine to 60″. Mark the centerline on the one-by-three, and start-

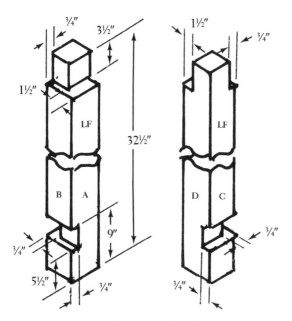

4-2.   *Leg, left front. (Courtesy of Stanley Tools.)*

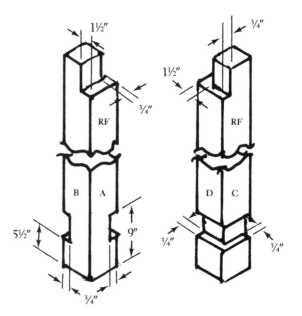

4-3.   *Leg, right front. (Courtesy of Stanley Tools.)*

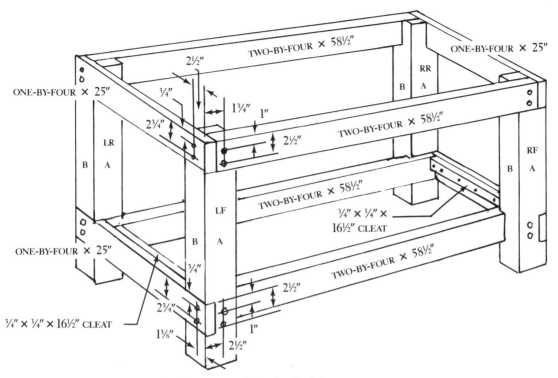

4-4. *Workbench frame assembly. (Courtesy of Stanley Tools.)*

ing from one end mark 10 points 2″ on center. Drill two ½″, five ¾″, and three 1″ holes at marked points. If you have needs that don't suit the size or number of holes, rearrange to suit. Clamp a scrap piece of one-by-three to the back of the piece being drilled to prevent splintering. Round-off the front corners with a coping saw, or a sander. Put the tool rack 2″ down on the one-by-twelve backboard, 6″ from each end. Mark bottom and end lines, remove rack, and mark screw locations every 12″, starting 2″ in from one end. Drill through backboard from the front, and attach the rack to the backboard with No. 8 × 1½″ screws.

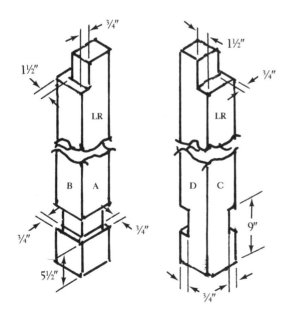

4-5. *Leg, left rear. (Courtesy of Stanley Tools.)*

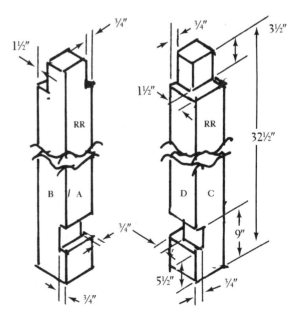

4-6. *Leg, right rear. (Courtesy of Stanley Tools.)*

17

Attach the backboard and tool rack to the framed pegboard, using 1¼″ No. 8 screws to attach to the backs of the front frame side pieces. The one-by-twelve will extend down 1½″ below the front frame side pieces. Square a line parallel to the backboard bottom, and ¾″ up. Drill for No. 10 screws, 6″ on center, starting 2″ in from an end.

Again, this next step requires help. Place the back assembly on the workbench, flush at both ends of the bench. Attach with 1½″ screws. This assembly will support itself, but not a load of tools.

Cut and attach two back support braces of two 23½″ and two 12″ pieces of one-by-four. Stack a 12″ piece on top of a 23½″ piece, butt one end, drill, and screw together with two No. 8 × 1¼″ screws. Place over backboard leg, flush with leg sides, making sure top butts against bottom of pegboard frame in back. It will not fit quite flush with the leg because of the carriage bolt heat. Hold firmly in place and tap solidly with a mallet to get impressions of bolt heads. Use 1″ bit to drill ¼″ deep holes to allow flush fit. Drill for No. 10 screws for leg attaching points, No. 8 for backboard. Attach to leg with three No. 10 × 3″ screws and to backboard with 1¼″ × No. 8 screws.

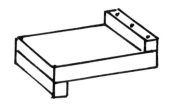

PRESS WORKPIECE AGAINST THE BACK STOP FOR STEADY, SQUARE HOLD.

4-8. *Bench hook. (Courtesy of Stanley Tools.)*

Add a middle support of a 16″ piece of one-by-four with two 1¼″ × No. 8 screws attaching it to a 1⅝″ wide × 16″ long piece of scrap pegboard. Make sure it's flush with bottom edge, and attach to the backboard, centered, by butting to the lip where the pegboard frame projects over the backboard. Use No. 8 × 1½″ screws. Sand edges and you're ready to go.

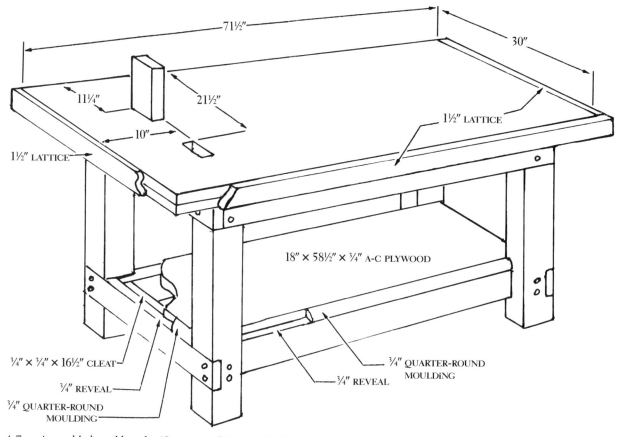

4-7. *Assembled workbench. (Courtesy of Stanley Tools.)*

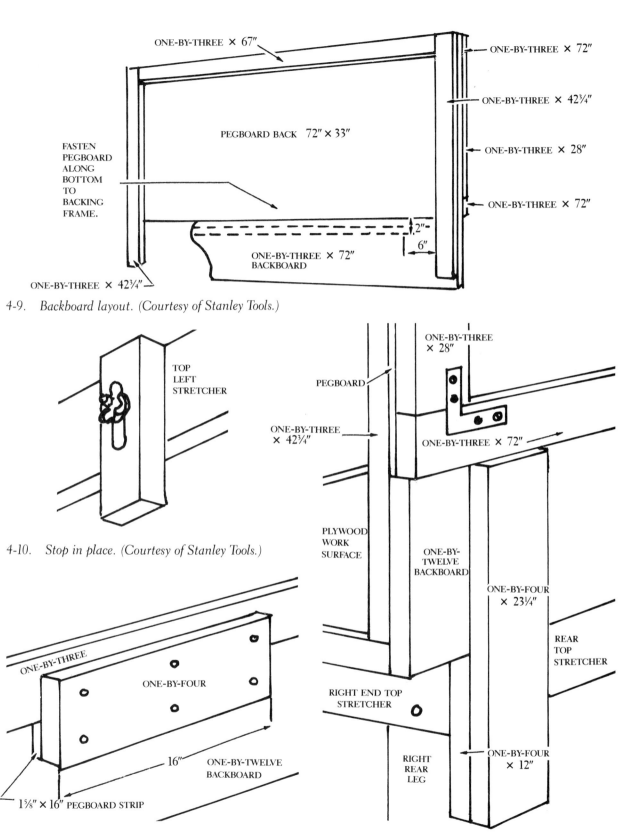

ONE-BY-THREE × 67″

ONE-BY-THREE × 72″

ONE-BY-THREE × 42¾″

ONE-BY-THREE × 28″

PEGBOARD BACK 72″ × 33″

ONE-BY-THREE × 72″

FASTEN PEGBOARD ALONG BOTTOM TO BACKING FRAME.

2″

6″

ONE-BY-THREE × 72″ BACKBOARD

ONE-BY-THREE × 42¾″

4-9. *Backboard layout. (Courtesy of Stanley Tools.)*

TOP LEFT STRETCHER

4-10. *Stop in place. (Courtesy of Stanley Tools.)*

ONE-BY-THREE × 28″

PEGBOARD

ONE-BY-THREE × 42¾″

ONE-BY-THREE × 72″

PLYWOOD WORK SURFACE

ONE-BY-TWELVE BACKBOARD

ONE-BY-FOUR × 23¼″

REAR TOP STRETCHER

RIGHT END TOP STRETCHER

RIGHT REAR LEG

ONE-BY-FOUR × 12″

ONE-BY-THREE

ONE-BY-FOUR

16″

ONE-BY-TWELVE BACKBOARD

1⅝″ × 16″ PEGBOARD STRIP

4-11. *Backboard center support. (Courtesy of Stanley Tools.)*

4-12. *Backboard end support. (Courtesy of Stanley Tools.)*

19

5-1.   *Sawhorse. (Courtesy of Stanley Tools.)*

5 ♦ Sawhorse

Sawhorses are essential to work that cannot be readily done in a workshop or other workbench-equipped spot. They're also handy in many workshops. If you want to make sawhorses for your shop or work area, you can use commercially available metal brackets or build a very functional sawhorse such as this one that features a shelf for keeping tools close at hand and off the floor. This version is stable, sturdy, and fairly fast to make. All measurements are for making a pair.

Materials
- 2″ × 6″ × 8′ (top)
- two 1″ × 6″ × 10′ (legs)
- ½″ or ¾″ A-C plywood, 24″ × 24″ or 12″ × 48″, scrap or leftovers
- two 1″ × 2″ × 10′ (stretchers)
- two ¾″ × 13″ × 24″ plywood (shelves)
- No. 8 × 1¼″ flathead Phillips screws
- No. 10 × 1½″ flathead Phillips screws

Tools
- square
- measuring tape
- clutched drill and driver bit
- handsaw
- circular saw
- dovetail or backsaw
- 1″ wood chisel
- plane
- hammer
- marking gauge

Start by cutting two 36″ pieces from the two-by-six stack. Lay out the tops, measuring in from each end 4″ and 9⅝″. Square lines across tops at both points. Turn on edge and mark a nine-degree angle on each line. Repeat at other end of top. Set marking gauge at ⁵⁄₁₆″ and scribe both sides of top between lines. Repeat for the second top (we're making a pair of sawhorses).

Make cuts for legs with a dovetail or backsaw. Be sure to hold proper angle, making the cut from the ⁵⁄₁₆″ depth on top face to no depth at the bottom face. Make relief cuts every ½″ along the cut, and use a 1″ chisel to remove material and smooth the depression.

Cut four 5′ lengths of one-by-six. Lay out a nine-degree angle ¼″ from the end of leg. Measure and mark 25⅝″ and lay out the second nine-degree angle. Turn the leg on edge and lay out a 10-degree angle. Repeat at other end of leg. The lines intersect with lines from the top surface. Use a handsaw to cut the compound angle. The cut forms the bottom of one leg and the top of the next, with all legs cut the same way. Screw hole placement differs. The cut is more easily made if you transfer the angle to a scrap block, and use the scrap block as a saw guide.

Screw four legs to each top piece, scribing a line ¾″ from the top of each leg. Mark screw locations at 1″, 3″, and 4¾″ along that line, and, with each leg flush with the top, drill and attach with No. 10 × 1½″ flathead Phillips screws. Measure, cut, and attach four end caps. The pieces start at 11½″ wide × 11¼″ high, with a centerline marked at 5¾″. Mark off to both sides of the centerline, 3⅝″ to each side and mark at the top. Draw a line from the bottom edge to the top mark on each side. Cut. This gives the angle. The finished piece is 7¼″ across the top, and serves as a pattern for the three other end caps you need.

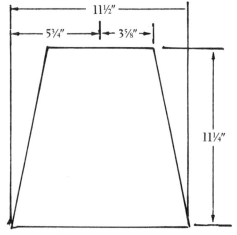

END CAP DIMENSIONS

5-2.   *End cap. (Courtesy of Stanley Tools.)*

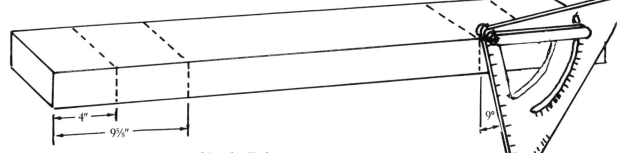

5-3. *Laying out angle. (Courtesy of Stanley Tools.)*

Screw in place with No. 8 screws, in drilled holes. The top two screws go in first, after which the legs are spread so they're flush with the end cap. The bottom screws go in then, and the center four screws go in last.

Cut four pieces of one-by-two to 36″ lengths. Mark each end at 12 degrees on both sides. You can now clamp in a vise and plane to the angle, or you can set a table saw and rip to the angle. Little enough material needs to be removed to make planing simple.

Fit each piece by placing against the side of the sawhorse, with bevel in right direction. Scribe angle on ends, and cut to fit.

Mark down ½″ from the top and ½″ up from the bottom. Mark screw hole locations at 2¾″ in on top line, and 1¼″ and 4½″ on the bottom line. Drill and screw in place with No. 8 × 1¼″ flathead Phillips screws.

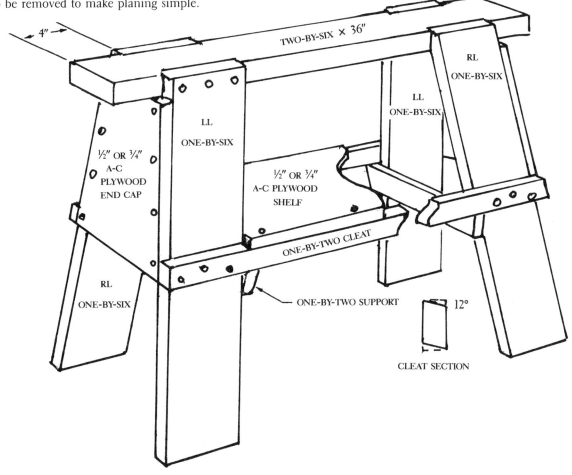

5-4. *Finished, with cleats in place. (Courtesy of Stanley Tools.)*

Cut two 12½″ × 20¼″ pieces of ½″ plywood. Drill three screw holes, for No. 8 screws, along the side edges of each piece, one 1″ from each end, and one at 10¼″. Attach with No. 8 × 1¼″ flathead Phillips screws. Bevel edges with plane to match cleat angle.

From one-by-two or one-by-three, cut four 13″ long leg braces. Mark the center point along one edge (6½″). Along the same edge, measure and mark 6⅛″ from center in both directions. Cut both ends off, cutting between the 6⅛″ and 6½″ marks. The result measures 13″ along the top edge and 12⁄14″ along the bottom end. Hold the 13″ edge up against the inside of legs on one end. Drill twice on each end for No. 8 × 1¼″ flathead Phillips screws. Screw those in, sand off any ragged edges, and your sawhorses are ready for use.

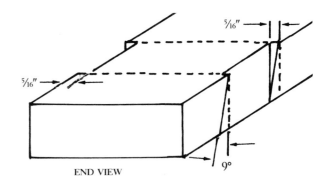

5-5. *Cutting angle. (Courtesy of Stanley Tools.)*

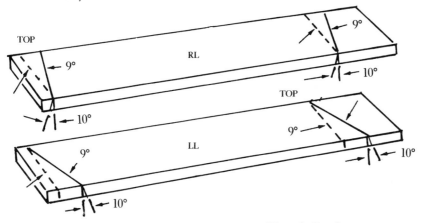

5-6. *Leg layout. (Courtesy of Stanley Tools.)*

Tool Care

Tool care is often common sense. Electrical tools must have good cords and unmangled plugs. Keep tools as clean as you can, and oil or otherwise lubricate those that need it. Use tools for the jobs for which they're made. The screwdriver always serves as an excellent example. Screwdrivers are to drive screws, and do okay at opening paint cans. They are not pry bars, chisels, or levers though everyone has used a screwdriver in those ways.

For special tools, follow the toolmakers' directions for tool care.

Tool Safety

Tool safety is also a matter of common sense, combined with some knowledge, with power tools particularly, of the ways in which tools and wood can react to force.

Always make sure you have a clear cutting line, and that tool cords can't snag as you cut. Snags mostly pull the cut off-line, but can cause a tool to be yanked loose from the cut and the hand. Keep your work area clear. Follow manufacturer's safety instructions for all tools. Always use safety devices, such as saw guards.

Wear eye protection, whether safety glasses, goggles, or a face shield. Use hearing protection against the cumulative effects of noise. *Think* before you work, and as you're working. Only *you* can assure such safety. If a procedure seems unsafe to you, *do not use it.*

2 · Outdoor Projects

There is a wide variety of outdoor projects that may be built, some easy to make, some far more complex. The uses are nearly as varied as the projects: sandboxes; picnic tables; occasional tables; benches; planters; chairs; lounges; and on.

Much depends on your own preferences and what you need. We start here with the simplest possible outdoor project. From there the mix of experience and time needed varies widely from project to project.

6 ◆ Sandbox

This large, but simple sandbox is set on a piece of patio cloth or at least 6 mil polyethylene, after construction. This keeps the sand from mixing with the dirt and tends to extend the time between refills. Patio cloth is best. Overlap that (it comes in 36″ width) on the 4′ direction.

Tools
- circular saw
- mitre saw, optional (use a slide type for the long 45-degree cuts)
- 16 oz. carpenter's hammer
- cordless drill and ⅛″ drill bit
- No. 2 Phillips screwdriver bit
- measuring tape
- square
- carpenter's pencil
- heavy-duty scissors, or utility knife

Materials
- three one-by-eight × 8′ pressure-treated pine
- two-by-six × 4′ pressure-treated pine
- 8d galvanized common nails
- 2″ galvanized coarse-thread Phillips screws
- 4′ × 6′ polyethylene, tarp, or patio cloth
- sand to fill (ours took 10 five-gallon bucketfuls)

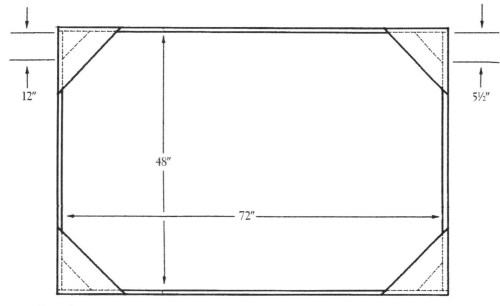

6-1. *Sandbox plan.*

Start by cutting one of the one-by-eights to produce two pieces, each 47¼" long. Then, cut two other pieces of one-by-eight, each 6' long.

Cut the two-by-six to form four triangles for the corners, with each side having a 45-degree cut. These are the screw-in braces for the corners: the cuts must be precise.

Nail the two 47¼" pieces inside the 6' long pieces, keeping edges as even as possible, so that a box 4' × 6' is formed. Screw the four corner braces in place, making sure they're even with the top edge of the box. Use 2" coarse-thread Phillips screws here.

Finally, cut the remaining pieces of one-by-eight to fit over the two-by-six corner braces and the sides. Screw these in place to form four corner seats. The cuts are, again, 45 degrees from the back edge to form a triangular corner set. Again, use the 2" drive screws, with coarse threads.

6-2. *The sandbox is partly filled, nearly ready for use.*

7 ◆ A-Frame Swing Set

This is quite possibly the most difficult project of all our "Quick & Easy" projects. It requires a minimum of two people, but is best done with three, at least during the erection of the large beam onto the A-frames.

The hardware units are available in different configurations, with various opportunities for starting play, and expansion. An infant seat is recommended for the youngest children. Always provide supervision whenever the set will be used, and do not allow any child heavier than 75 lbs. to use the equipment.

Materials
- hardware set
- two-by-four × 10' (all lumber must be pressure-treated)
- two-by-six × 8'
- two two-by-six × 10'
- two two-by-six × 12'
- six four-by-four × 8'
- four-by-six × 16' (or laminated two-by-six × 16')
- 16d galvanized nails
- 10d galvanized nails

Begin the process by checking the site to make sure you've got sufficient free space for safe use of the swing set—a 6' to 8' use zone all the way around the set. This means a free space of no less than 28' long and 20' deep (with more for when the slide is added, and even more for when the monkey bars are added). Obviously, no power or phone lines may be allowed to be even close to within the use area.

7-1. *The A-frame play set, ready for use.*

Check construction as you go along. No inverted angles are allowed (such angles can catch children). Make sure a 10" diameter ball will pass through all openings (rails, etc.).

Tools
- ½", or heavy-duty ⅜", electric drill, ⅛" drill bit, and ⅜" drill bit (at least 6", or preferably 12", in exposed length)
- circular saw
- handsaw (8 or 10 points per inch)
- 16' tape measure
- 20 oz. claw hammer
- adjustable wrench
- pliers
- large square

Cut lumber as follows: do *not* cut the four-by-sixes or the four-by-fours; cut three 35″ pieces from the two-by-four × 10′; cut two 28″ and one 35″ piece from the two-by-six × 8′; cut four 28″ pieces from one two-by-six × 10′; cut a 72″ cross-brace, and a 35″ piece from the next two-by-six × 10′; cut three 28″ and two 25″ pieces from the two-by-six × 12′; then cut two 53″ and one 35″ piece from the last two-by-six × 12′.

After that, it's assembly time. The deck frame goes together first, coming in 6″ from the ends of the two 53″ two-by-sixes. Use a square to draw the line. Drill pilot holes, and nail two 25″ two-by-sixes inside those 6″ lines. Once nailing is done, make sure the frame is square. You may use the square to check, but making sure diagonal measurements are equal is just as fast, and possibly easier. Adjust as needed.

Lay the nine 28″ two-by-sixes on top of the frame, and space equally. Drill pilot holes, and use two 16d nails per end to cover the deck frame.

Check the lengths of the 8′ four-by-fours. Lumberyard-fresh lengths may vary as much as 2″, usually in extra length. Lay two of the four-by-fours on the lawn, or drive with two ends together in an angle (drive is preferable if you don't have to move the finished assembly too far afterwards). Use eight 10d nails to assemble the two four-by-fours and the frame bracket.

Set the frame base at 94½″ wide (to the outsides of the legs), measure up 26″ on each leg, and nail the 72″ cross-member in place, using four 16d nails in each leg. Drill pilot holes.

7-2. *Stan is nailing the A-frame support in place.*

7-3. *Here, the deck is nailed to one side of the A-frame.*

Make two more A-frames, without the cross-braces, and make sure the bases are 94½″ apart. Measure up 48″ along the insides of all four legs and mark. With one A-frame lying on the ground, set the deck assembly in place, lining the bottom of the deck assembly up with the 48″ marks. Drill pilot holes and nail in place with four 16d nails at each leg.

Repeat the process with the second leg assembly. Here, the third person is quite helpful, as the leg assembly is just balanced on the deck, and tends to teeter out of line with its marks. With person number three holding the top end, no teetering occurs.

Steps are added on one side, using two-by-fours (they go on the left as the end of the A-frame assembly faces you, with the two-by-sixes applied on the right side—for the future slide, Project 8). Nail, to the tops of the two-by-fours, 13″ from the bottom of the leg, 26½″ from the bottom of the leg, and 40″ from the bottom of the leg. On the opposite side, nail the first two-by-six 14½″ to the top of the two-by-six, from the bottom of the leg, the next at 30″, and the last at 45½.″ Use 16d nails, three at each junction.

Prepare to work on the four-by-six × 16′ piece (or the laminated two-by-six × 16′). You will need to chuck the long ⅜″ drill bit for the following holes. Set a combination square at 1¾″ (half the width of the four-by-six, which is actually 3½″ wide after drying and planing). Measure, and mark along the middle of the beam, 2″, 7½″, 23½″, 39½″, 56½″, 72½″, 89½″, 105½″, 121½″, 127″, 153″, and 158½″. These marks must be accurate, with special attention paid to those marking the junctions with the A-frames (2″ and 7½″; 121½″ and 127″; 153″ and 158½″). Half an inch here or there for the hangers for the swings, seats, and rings doesn't much matter, but come up short or long on the holes that have to align with the frame brackets, and you've got a lot of fiddling to do, and some fresh drilling from positions that are not a lot of fun.

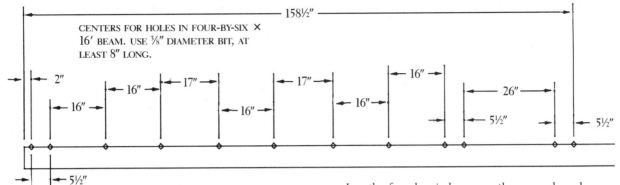

158½"

CENTERS FOR HOLES IN FOUR-BY-SIX ✕ 16' BEAM. USE ⅜" DIAMETER BIT, AT LEAST 8" LONG.

2"

16"   16"   17"   17"   16"

16"   16"   16"   26"

5½"   5½"

5½"

7-4. *Beam hole layout drawing.*

7-5. *Stan drills the four-by-six while Kathy looks on impatiently.*

Assemble the hangers on the beam, with the top beam clamp having the round hole, and the bottom clamp the oval hole. Hangers use ⁵⁄₁₆" washers and lock nuts. Nail the plates in place with four 10d nails each, too. Do the nailing *after* the hangers are inserted, so that you're dead sure upper and lower plates line up properly. Pop the carriage bolts temporarily through the upper plates and into the beam before nailing the top plates on those (those don't have lower plates, as they go through the frame brackets). You can leave all of that assembly until the carriage bolts go through, if you wish.

Lay the four-by-six beam on the ground, and move the single A-frame into place, assembling with the carriage bolt and lock nut (the carriage bolt goes through from underneath).

Now we're at the point where three people are almost essential. The beam and single A-frame is lifted into place, with the doubled A-frame/deck assembly unit already in place. The beam is quite unwieldy at this point, and until at least one carriage bolt is loosely in place on a deck assembly A-frame, there is some danger of damage to the components if it slips and twists.

Get at least one more carriage bolt in place, with the nut started, but not tightened. Now, run in the final carriage bolt and tighten that nut. Tighten the other nut. Check all fastenings, and go along and make sure all plates are secured with four 10d nails.

Swing seats need to be assembled. Thread the side chains through the tunnels moulded into the seat bottoms, until a full link shows at each end. The harnesses attach to these, with the open ends clamped shut with pliers. Then the vinyl-covered chain is checked for height. The vinyl cover is trimmed back to allow height adjustment, and the chains are installed, and open links closed with the pliers. The same adjustments are made to the rings. The infant seat doesn't require adjustment, and is hung with polypropylene ropes.

8 ♦ Slide Assembly

The basic problem with projects such as the above is keeping the kids away while you're working on them. To add some more fun to your A-frame swing set, and to make the job even more enjoyable, select a galvanized slide kit that needs a bit of assembly.

Materials
- galvanized slide kit
- three two-by-four ✕ 8' pressure-treated Southern pine
- 10d galvanized nails

Tools

- circular saw
- square
- measuring tape
- 20 oz. hammer
- drill, ³⁄₁₆″ and ⅛″ drill bit

Start by cutting two of the two-by-fours to 91″ lengths. Next, cut four 16⅛″ lengths, and a single 19″ length.

Nail two of the 16⅛″ supports between the two-by-four × 91″ lengths, resulting in a 19″ wide box. The slide is then lowered over the box sides, and the ³⁄₁₆″ drill bit used to drill through the sides of the metal and into the frame. At these points, the remaining two 16⅛″ pieces are nailed, with nails going through the metal and the wood sides and into the supports.

Finally, the 19″ slide support is nailed on, 1″ down from the top end of the slide.

The slide we used has a kickout, and requires a two-by-six frame to keep it from running into the ground. That is made to fit inside the bottom end, in place of one 16⅛″ support.

Once the kids get used to the slide, you might want to lay on a couple of coats of good paste auto wax to speed things up.

9 ♦ Cargo Net

The cargo net is another fun-filled addition you can make to your A-Frame Swing Set (Project 7). It is simple to add and will provide endless enjoyment for the kids.

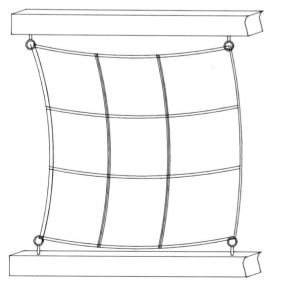

9-1.   *Cargo net.* See also *Illus. 7-1.*

Materials

- 60″ four-by-four
- cargo net
- two ⁵⁄₁₆″ × 8″ carriage bolts, nuts, and washers

The cargo net requires only the net itself, with supplied fasteners, and a section of four-by-four lumber that is run across the bottom of the two deck A-frames of the swing set (Project 7). The upper A-frame bolt is removed from the last frame bracket, and two other holes (⅜″, using the 12″ long drill bit) are drilled.

The supports are installed and bolted in place, and holes are drilled through the four-by-four, where the bottom two supports are installed.

The net is now in place. It will probably terrify most children the first couple of times they climb it. Parents who want to avoid equal terror will probably want to set down the rules right away, and not let the kids use the upper bar as a balance beam after they clamber up the net.

10 ♦ Bluebird House No. 1

This is simple to make, a useful project that goes together in just a few minutes. This design (and Projects 11 and 12) is similar to one used by various birding associations, but is my own adaptation. I made mine of redwood, but it could also be made of cedar. Pine, poplar, and similar woods need paint to survive any length of time outdoors, but might be used.

10-1.   *Bluebird house.*

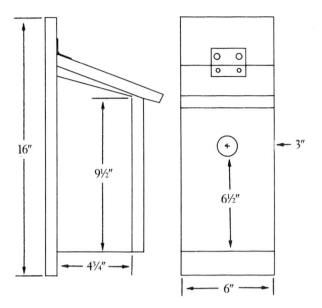

10-2. *Bluebird house drawing.*

Materials
- ¾" × 6" × 16" redwood
- two ¾" × 6" × 10½" (back, angled to 9½" at front) redwood for sides
- two ¾" × 6" × 9½" redwood, bevelled 10 degrees at top, for front and lid
- ¾" × 4½" × 6" redwood (floor)
- brass screw insert
- ½" brass thumbscrew
- solid brass hinge, 2" × 1¾"
- 6d galvanized finishing nails

Tools
- combination square
- measuring tape
- saw
- drill, and 1½'', ¼", ⅜" drill bit
- drill bit to fit screw insert
- 13 or 16 oz. claw hammer
- nail set

Start by checking all pieces for square, and then assemble the box—sides, inside front, and back—using the 6d galvanized nails. Install the sides about 2½" down from the top of the back (the oversize back provides area for you to screw or nail the nesting box to a fence post, etc.). Install the floor next, using the same type of nails. Drill a ⅜" hole in each corner of the floor once it is nailed in place. This provides drainage. Drill at least three ⅜" holes near the top of each side for ventilation.

Install the top, with the single hinge centered. Then mark the back the correct distance, and drill a ¼" hole through the top *only*. Mark the center of that hole in the

upper edge of the front. Drill to accept the screw insert, and check fit of thumbscrew.

Hang the bluebird house and wait. I made six of these last year, and hung five around my house. Only one went up early enough to draw a family, but now we have three times as many bluebirds as we had the preceding year. Next year, the rest should be occupied, further increasing the area's Eastern bluebird population.

Hang the nesting box about chest high (4', give or take a bit), near a brushy area or low tree.

I didn't finish any of mine, but a coat of clear water repellent will add some years to useful life. The lift-up top makes for an easy clean-out each fall.

11 ♦ Bluebird House No. 2

A second version varies only in the use of a short board (1¼" × ¾" × 5", redwood) replacing the hinge. Place the board with the top in place, and nail to hold the top firmly, without jamming. You can further simplify the construction by removing the brass screw-in thread and thumbscrew. To do this, use epoxy adhesive to glue on two ¾" × ½" × 4" redwood cleats spaced on the front bottom side of the lid so that they grip the front of the box firmly.

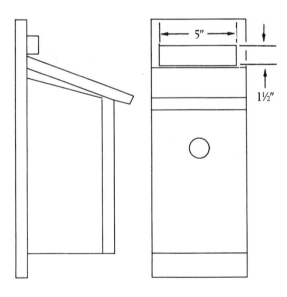

DIMENSIONS IDENTICAL TO BLUEBIRD HOUSE NO. 1, EXCEPT FOR CLEAT

11-1. *Bluebird house drawing.*

12 ◆ Bluebird House No. 3

The third version offers a differently tapered side that requires no ventilation hole drilling. The basic difference is simple. Make the side the same height, front and back: that is, the side is cut square, instead of 9½" at the front and 10½" at the back. The top is set at the same

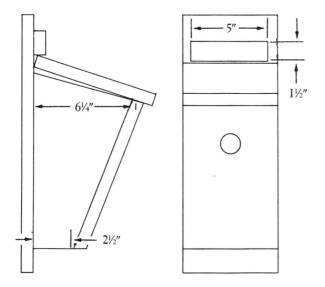

12-1. Tapered side bluebird house drawing.

height (10½"), leaving a tapering 1" back-to-front gap for ventilation. This removes one drilling step from construction, making the birdhouse even simpler to build.

13 ◆ Wren House

My wren house is another simple pattern. It differs from the bluebird house primarily in side and roof design, and in entry hole size.

Materials
- ¾" × 6" × 14" redwood
- two ¾" × 6" × 9½" (top side tapers from 9" at front to 9½" at back) redwood for sides
- two ¾" × 6" × 9½" redwood, bevelled 10 degrees at top (front and lid)
- ¾" × 4½" × 4" redwood (floor)
- solid brass hinge, 2" × 1¾"
- 6d galvanized finishing nails

Cut boards to starting size, and then set the table-saw rip fence up so that the taper jig will cut off ½" at one end of the 8½" boards, and nothing at the other end. Cut a single side taper on each of the side boards.

Nail the untapered side of the side boards to the back board, 2" down from the top. Nail the front onto the tapered sides of the boards.

Check the fit of the bottom, and do *not* correct for front taper: there should be a ¼" gap at the front of the floor where it doesn't quite meet the front of the nesting box. This allows drainage.

Place the top, and adjust to accept the hinge. Install the hinge, and make two ¾" × 1" × 4" long cleats. Nail and glue these (with epoxy) to the underside of the top front, where they grip the front to prevent inadvertent opening of the nesting box, while allowing for easy clean-out.

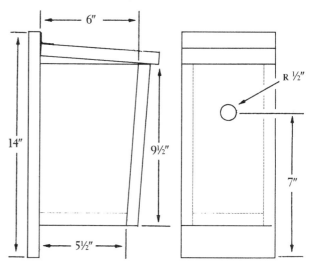

13-1. Wren house drawing.

All nesting boxes must be cleaned once a year. Doing the job in winter solves problems with wasps that also use the nesting boxes.

Tools
- combination square
- measuring tape
- saw
- taper jig
- drill, and ¼" drill bit
- 1" drill bit (entry hole—use 1⅛" for Carolina wrens)
- drill bit to fit screw insert (probably ⁷⁄₁₆", but check first)
- 13 or 16 oz. claw hammer
- nail set

14-1.   Decorations for a birdhouse—doors and windows.

14 ◆ Decorated Birdhouse

This birdhouse, of redwood or pine, uses decorative doors and windows as accents to add attractiveness, and to make the birdhouse different from those already in place. The basic birdhouse is simple to make, starting with a standard eaved roof, and going to a pivoting floor.

Materials

- two one-by-six × 6″ redwood (sides)
- two one-by-eight × 10″ redwood (front and back)
- two one-by-eight × 8″ redwood (roof)
- one-by-eight × 5½″ redwood (floor)
- 6d galvanized nails
- 8d galvanized finishing nails
- 1½″ knurled handle brass machine screw
- ½″ brass screw thread insert
- white exterior paint
- asphalt roofing shingles
- two plastic windows
- plastic door
- dark blue spray paint

Tools

- 8- or 10-tooth saw
- power mitre box (or careful use of square with above saw)
- square
- measuring tape
- hammer
- screwdriver
- drill, and drill bits for knurled screw, for brass screw insert, and for entry hole
- nail set
- 2″ paintbrush

Start by cutting all materials to size, as above, with the front and back cut with a 45-degree roof mitre, with a centered peak.

Assemble the sides inside the front and back, and install the roof along the eave lines. Insert the floor for a test fit, and drill the hole for the knurled handle screw into the lower edge of one side, off-center when compared back to front. Mark the center of the screw insert through this hole.

Remove the floor and drill for the screw insert. Install the insert. Replace the floor and use two 8d galvanized nails as center pivots for the floor. Before placing the knurled screw, paint the entire assembly (except the rooftop) white. Spray-paint one side of doors and windows dark blue.

Install the asphalt shingles with waterproof glue. Glue doors and windows in place, using epoxy glue, after scraping off a bit of paint under the doors and windows (so the epoxy will adhere better).

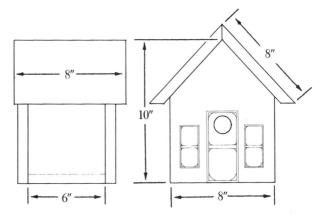

14-2.   Drawing of decorated birdhouse.

Drill the entry hole inside the upper door opening. Here are some suggestions depending on what kind of bird you want to attract: 1″ for nuthatches, 1⅛″ for chickadees, 1¼″ for titmice, and 1½″ for bluebirds.

Install the knurled screw so that the floor will *not* pivot. When the knob is turned, the screw may be pulled out, and the floor pivoted around its 8d nails for cleaning.

15 ◆ Bird Feeder

Some of our feeders were showing definite signs of having been used too long. I took the opportunity to develop a new pattern. This one is made of red cedar instead of redwood, as some of my patterns in earlier books are.

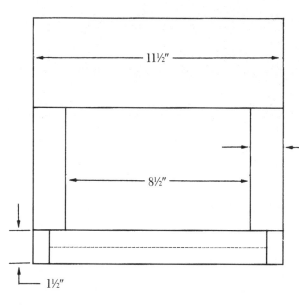

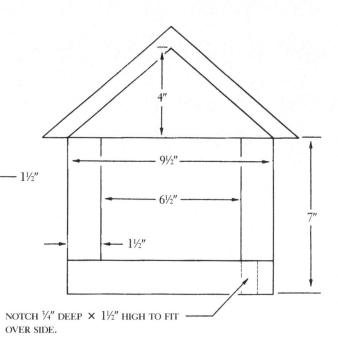

NOTCH ¾″ DEEP × 1½″ HIGH TO FIT
OVER SIDE.

15-1.   Bird feeder drawing.

Materials
(wood stock ¾″ thick unless specified)
- 6″ × 10″ cedar (roof half)
- 5¼″ × 10″ cedar (roof half)
- two 6″ × 8″ cedar (eave ends, angle cut to fit inside of roof)
- four 1½″ × 1½″ × 10″ (corner posts)
- 10″ × 8″ cedar (floor)
- two 1½″ × 10″ cedar (sides)
- two 1½″ × 11½″ cedar (sides)
- 6d galvanized finishing nails
- two solid-brass hinges, 2″ × 1¾″
- resorcinol or epoxy glue

Tools
- saw
- drill
- vix bit (to fit hinge screws)
- mitre box (to slant posts to fit roof line)
- 13 or 16 oz. claw hammer

Glue up the floor and roof boards as needed. Cut to final size. Assemble, with resorcinol or epoxy glue and galvanized finishing nails, sides on bottom. Notch and assemble posts, after cutting top to fit angle of eaves. Add eave boards to the posts. Nail and glue the widest roof board in place, and attach the narrower roof board to that with hinges. Use brass cabinet hooks to hold in place at lower edge.

The feeder can be mounted on a post, or hung from a tree with rope or wire.

16 ◆ Frontier Fort

The pattern for this "Frontier Fort" is easily followed. It uses four-by-four timbers (the one shown used four-by-six, an unnecessary expense), and an old, small cable reel (to form a step into the fort).

16-1.   Frontier fort. (Courtesy of Wolmanized Wood.)

Materials
(all lumber four-by-four pressure-treated stock)
- (eighteen 8′ (three sides)
- thirty 8′ (floor, last layer of foundation)

- six 3½′ (one side of door side of fort)
- sixteen 4′ (foundation underpinning)
- six 2′ (second side of door side of fort)
- sixteen 1′ (top caps, and spacers at "door")
- four 12″ galvanized spikes
- eighty 6″ spikes
- empty cable reel (about 3′ diameter, 12″ to 16″ height)

Tools
- chain saw or circular saw for deep cuts
- 28 oz. framing hammer
- framing square
- measuring tape, 12′
- heavy-duty electric drill, ⅜″ × 12″, and ³⁄₁₆″ × 6″ bits

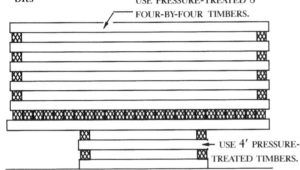

16-2. *Drawing of fort.*

Start by cutting all lumber to the above sizes.

Lay out the basic ground pattern, leaving at least a 2″ overlap on each end of square posts. Two posts go on the ground, parallel. Two more go on top of those, at right angles, and parallel to each other. The process is then repeated, giving a total of four thicknesses high. Each of these is spiked with 6″ spikes at the corners. Drill ³⁄₁₆″ pilot holes for spikes, and make sure corners are square.

On top of the described base, lay four full-length (8′) four-by-fours. These are spiked down with four 6″ spikes for each four-by-four. Start the floor layer on these timbers, starting 6″ in from each end, and leaving ⅛″ of space between each four-by-four on the floor (a 16d nail is about ⅛″ thick, so several of those make good spacers). Spike with 6″ spikes at each crossing point, after drilling pilot holes.

With the floor in place, start the side walls, laying base members parallel on two sides, at right angles to the beams under the floor. Lay the wall members 6″ in from the outside edges of the 8′-long floor members. Spike at corners, as above. On the second row (at right angles to the first row of two) use 12″ spikes.

Raise the wall to the height you've decided. I recommend no less than five four-by-fours high, and no more than six high. That's sufficient to be waist high, or nearly so, to the age groups of children most interested in this kind of frontier fort. Spike each row at its corners into the row below, using 6″ spikes.

Roll the cable reel into place to serve as an entry. If no cable reel can be found, use a set of stairs, made of three four-step stair stringers, and 4′ wide two-by-sixes for treads—two two-by-sixes per tread.

17 ◆ Southern Pine Bench

This quick-to-make bench is of pressure-treated Southern pine. I suggest using wood that is for in-ground use and that has been treated to add water repellency.

Materials
- two-by-twelve × 10′ stock
- two-by-twelve × 8′ stock
- eleven two-by-four × 6′ stock
- eight ⁵⁄₁₆″ × 3″ galvanized lag screws
- twelve ⁵⁄₁₆″ × 4″ galvanized lag screws
- 10d and 12d galvanized common nails
- neoprene (hard rubber) to make forty-five 3½″ squares, ¼″ thick
- construction adhesive (that works with pressure-treated lumber)

Tools
- circular or crosscut saw
- hammer
- ½″ box or socket wrench
- drill, ¼″ bit
- square
- tape measure

17-1. *Southern pine bench. (Courtesy of the Southern Forest Products Association.)*

Start by cutting pieces to length, as follows: one 5′ 8″ piece and six 6¼″ pieces from the long (10′) two-by-twelve. Produce center supports according to the drawing using the shorter pieces. Use the shorter two-by-twelve to make another 5′ 8″-long piece and four more 6¼″ long pieces. The four short pieces become *end* supports, as drawn. Cut three 11¼″ pieces, and two 17¼″ pieces. The remaining 10 two-by-fours are all cut to 5′ 8″ length.

Fabricate the two vertical support assemblies, marking the location of all end and center supports on the 5′ 8″-long two-by-twelves. To ease lag screw installation, tack each support in place with a 10d nail. Drill ¼″ holes through the two-by-twelve into the end and center supports. Use the wrench to install two 3″ lag screws in each end support and two 4″ lag screws in each center support.

Position three two-by-four spacers, 11¼″ long, between vertical support assemblies. Nail all three spacers to one assembly, with 10d nails. Line up two vertical assemblies and fasten together with 12d nails and construction adhesive.

Build the frame of the seating deck, using two two-by-fours, each 17¼″ long, to the ends of two two-by-fours each 5′ 8″ long. Use 10d nails and construction adhesive. Drill nail holes with a ⅛″ or 3/16″ drill bit. Check frame for square.

Arrange eight two-by-fours vertically within the frame, using ¼″ neoprene spacers between them. Secure spacers (in line with center and end supports) with construction adhesive. Nail all of the two-by-fours through the end two-by-fours of the frame. Use 10d nails and construction adhesive for greatest strength. Check square again.

Run a bead of construction adhesive across the top edges of all two-by-twelve vertical, end, and center supports. Align seat deck as shown. Only the two two-by-four frame ends will overhang. Use 12d nails to toe-nail seating deck to support assembly. Use one nail through the deck side into each center support.

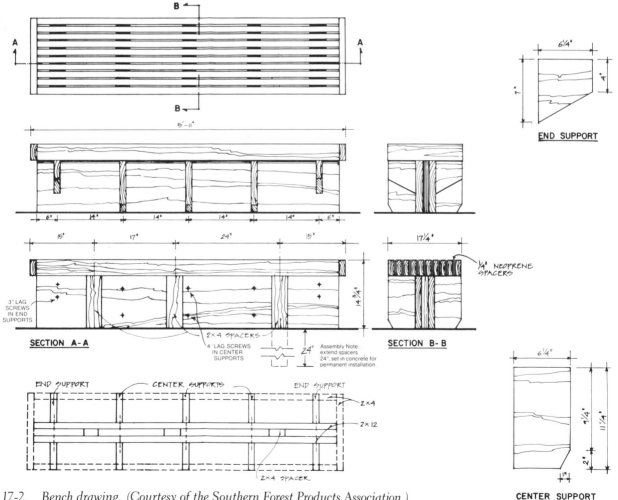

17-2. *Bench drawing. (Courtesy of the Southern Forest Products Association.)*

18 ◆ Trash Can and Firewood Storage

Most storage units hide trash cans well, but leave firewood exposed to the rain—and snow, and sleet. This, of Southern pine, covers both.

Materials

(all wood is pressure-treated Southern pine, standard 0.25 retention unless indicated)

- two-by-four × 8' (ground contact, 0.40 retention desirable)
- six two-by-four × 12' (ground contact, 0.40 retention desirable)
- two two-by-four × 10'
- two-by-four × 12'
- two two-by-two × 6'
- three 4' × 8' × ½" T1-11 siding
- 6d galvanized nails
- 10d galvanized nails
- two pair 3" galvanized butt hinges with screws
- door handle, or lock and hasp (as desired)
- construction adhesive (for pressure-treated wood)
- 4' × 8' × ½" CDX plywood
- roofing felt, 15 or 30 lb.
- fibreglass shingles, one bundle (33⅓ sq ft)
- 1" roofing nails
- galvanized roof ridge, 6'

Tools
- level
- square
- measuring tape
- circular saw
- handsaw
- hammer
- screwdriver

Cut the wood as follows: from the 8' two-by-four, cut three bottom frame supports, 2' 2½" long each; from one of the 12' two-by-fours, cut two pieces 3' 10½" long, and two pieces 1' 9" long. From another long two-by-four (0.40), cut two rear corner posts 4' 1" long, plus one front corner post 3' 3" long. Refer to drawing for roof slope and cut post tops to match. From another 12' two-by-four (0.40), cut front and rear center supports 3' 8" long and 2' 11" long, respectively. Notch them at the top to receive a two-by-four brace. Cut the other front corner post 3' 3" long. From the only 12' two-by-four treated to 0.25, cut front and rear top supports 5' 9" long.

18-1. Trash can and firewood storage. (Courtesy of the Southern Forest Products Association.)

From each of the two 10' two-by-fours, cut two rafters, 3' 4" long, and one end brace 2' 2½" long. Refer to drawing to get roof slope and notching needs.

Construct the two-by-four frame according to the plan, using 10d nails and construction adhesive. Check for level and square.

Locate the end braces and attach to corner posts with 10d nails. Read of end brace must be flush with rear corner posts, as in drawing. Install two-by-four top supports (front and rear), fitting to the notched center posts. Nail to center posts and toe-nail to corner posts. End-nail front support to braces. All is done with 10d nails and construction adhesive.

Keep a running check on level and square.

Use scrap two-by-four for blocking between end braces and rear top supports. Attach blocking to corner posts using 10d nails. Toe-nail rafters in place, evenly spacing them across span of top supports. Use 10d nails and construction adhesive. End rafter may also be attached to corner posts.

Cut a panel of treated plywood to 4' × 6'. Attach to rear with 6d nails and construction adhesive. Tops of panel and posts must be flush.

Cut six floor deck boards from the three remaining 12' two-by-fours (0.40 retention). Notch front and rear members as needed around center posts. Position floor deck pieces 1" apart, and recess the front member ½" to allow for the door. Nail to bottom framing with 10d nails and construction adhesive.

Cut treated panels to fit sides. Attach to frame and rafter with 6d nails and construction adhesive. Cut a square panel, 2' 4" on a side, from the treated plywood, to make a divider panel. Attach to center posts with 6d nails and adhesive.

Build the doors. Cut two treated-plywood sections 1' 10¾" × 2' 3" high each. Attach the two-by-two frame to the doors with 6d nails and adhesive. Frame is flush with plywood on three edges, with siding extending 2" below the bottom to clear the floor deck.

Attach doors to posts with butt hinges. Make a door stop of plywood, and attach to support with 6d nails and adhesive.

Install the ½" sheathing on the roof with 6d nails and adhesive. Cover with roofing felt, and then with shingles, aligning and nailing shingles as the manufacturer directs.

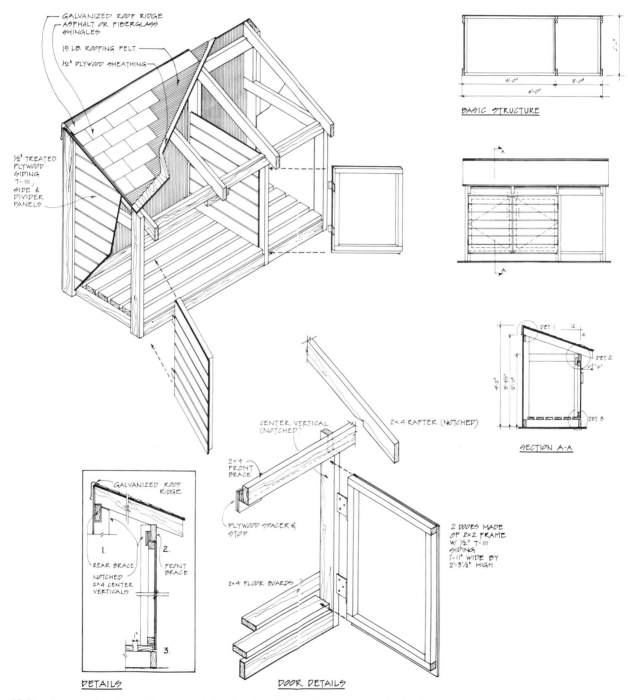

18-2. *Storage drawing. (Courtesy of the Southern Forest Products Association.)*

19 ♦ Redwood Planter

Redwood is pleasant to work with, especially for planter applications. This easy-to-make planter works well on decks and in most backyards.

Materials
- two-by-six × 10′ (construction heart redwood)
- one-by-ten × 10′ (common)
- two-by-four × 10′ (heart)
- one-by-ten × 16′ (heart)
- two-by-four × 6′ (heart)
- four heavy-duty casters, 2½″
- 10d and 6d galvanized or aluminum nails
- 4d galvanized nails
- construction adhesive and gun

Tools
- circular saw or power mitre box
- hammer
- measuring tape
- square
- drill, ½″ and ⅛″ drill bit
- screwdriver

Cut four pieces of one-by-ten at 30″ lengths, and six at 33″. You'll also need two one-by-ten × 36″ and five two-by-six × 3′ lengths. Two two-by-four × 30″ serve as bottom rests, for attaching the casters. You also need four two-by-four × 17″ for corner braces, with tops bevelled at about 30 degrees.

Nail the floor pieces of two-by-six (30″) to the two-by-four floor bracing with 10d nails. Drill pilot holes to prevent splitting. Notch corner two-by-sixes to fit around

19-1. *Redwood planter. (Courtesy of the California Redwood Association.)*

the two-by-four upright corner braces. Nail the first 30″ one-by-ten along the bottom, with the bottom edge of the one-by-ten flush with the bottom edge of the two-by-four floor brace. Repeat the process on the opposite side. Add the lower two end 33″ one-by-tens, and then nail in the corner braces. Use 12 nails for nailing, and make sure to drill pilot holes. Nail on upper rows of 30″ and 33″ one-by-tens. For the final touch on the trim, nail on the one-by-ten × 36″ and one-by-ten × 33″ trim pieces centered on the sides (up 4⅝″ from the bottom) with 4d nails and construction adhesive.

Screw on the casters in each corner, after drilling pilot holes for the screws. Drill ½″ holes near each corner (at least eight) for drainage.

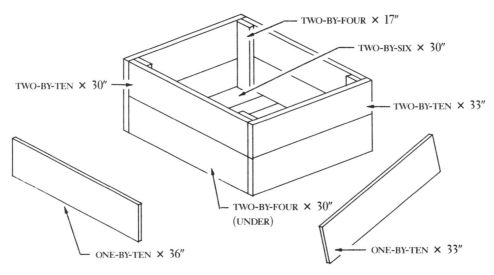

19-2. *Planter drawing.*

3 · Super-Quick Projects

Some projects are more "quick & easy" than are others. These are among the fastest possible, requiring, usually, less than three hours to complete, including time to sand and apply the first coat of finish.

20 ◆ Windy Day Napkin Holder

Constructed of three small pieces of cedar and two ¾″ × 6″ dowels, this napkin holder has a sliding center bar that sits on paper napkins, keeping them in place when the family eats outdoors.

Materials
- ¾″ × 6″ × 10″ cedar
- ¾″ × 2″ × 10″ cedar
- ¾″ × 1⅞″ × 10″ cedar
- two ¾″ × 6″ birch dowels
- wood glue

Tools
- measuring tape
- combination square
- saw
- drill, with ¾″, and ⅞″ or 1″ Forstner drill bits
- two bar clamps
- sandpaper

Start by cutting the cedar pieces from any cedar board large enough to produce them. Make sure the grain runs the *long* way on all pieces.

Mark in 1″ from each end on the two narrow cedar pieces, and half the distance (1″ and ¹⁵⁄₁₆″) across each piece. Drill a ¾″ flat-bottomed hole in the narrow (1⅞″) piece. Drill a ⅞″ or 1″ hole all the way through the wider (2″) piece.

Drill a flat-bottomed ¾″ hole at points 1″ in and centered on the base piece (6″ × 10″)—that is, 3″ in from either side. All flat-bottomed holes should be ⅜″ deep.

Spread glue on dowels and in holes, and insert dowels in the base, first. Place the slide (2″ × 10″ with larger holes) next. Finally, insert the dowels in the flat-bottomed holes in the 1⅞″ wide top. Clamp.

Sand lightly and finish, as desired.

The very slightly wider sliding part, with oversize holes, means it won't jam up and will be easy to grip to move up or down on a fresh pack of napkins.

20-1.   *Sliding bar holds napkins.*

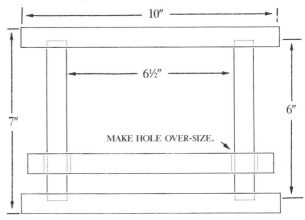

20-2.   *Napkin holder drawing.*

21 ♦ Kidney-Shaped Stool

This stool uses four turned legs and an 18″ × 11½″ piece of poplar that started life as a rough-cut board 12″ wide and 2¼″ thick. Planing brought it down to 1⅞″ thick. Holes were drilled in 1½″ from each short edge and 2″ from each long edge. The holes, ¾″ in diameter and flat-bottomed, accepted the ¾″ tenons on the already turned legs.

Materials
- four turned legs
- poplar board, 12″ × 2″
- woodworking glue

Tools
- measuring tape
- combination square
- drill, ¾″ Forstner bit
- coping, scroll, or band saw
- saw for straight cuts
- router, ⅜″ ogive bit
- sandpaper

Instead of clamping the legs, individually, when gluing up this stool (or any similar project), simply stand the stool upright on a flat surface and stack about 70 lbs. of tools, books, or anything else on top. It may also be clamped to the bench top. Apply glue to the tenon sides and to the hole, using a cheap brush, or other spreader, to make sure the glue is even all around. Once the glue is set, finish as desired.

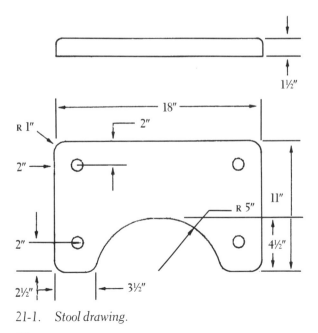

21-1.   *Stool drawing.*

21-2.   *Kidney-shaped stool.*

21-3.   *Rounded edges.*

22 ♦ Rectangular Stool

This stool, similar to that above, is even easier to make, as there is no curved cut.

Materials
- four turned hardwood legs
- 12″ × 18″ × 2″ poplar board
- woodworking glue

Tools
- measuring tape
- combination square
- drill, ¾″ Forstner bit
- router, ⅜″ round-over bit
- saw
- sandpaper

22-1. *Rectangular stool.*

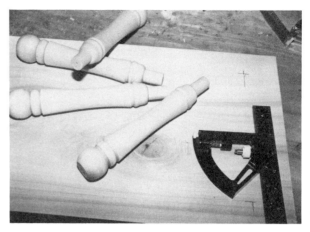

22-3. *Mark holes for legs.*

Holes are drilled in 1½″ from the short edge of the board and 2″ from the long edge. The edges are rounded with a router and ⅜″ round-over bit, after the corners are sanded to shape.

Glue is applied to tenon sides and to the hole sides and bottom, and the tenons are installed.

Place weights on top of the stool and give it a few hours for the glue to set. Finish as desired, with paint, or clear finish over stain (I don't always like to use stains, but when woods are different species, stains greatly enhance uniformity of appearance).

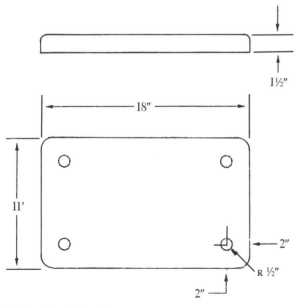

22-2. *Stool drawing.*

23 ◆ Three-Legged Stool

This is a slightly different design, one that started out as a circular three-legged, more or less classic, stool, but changed halfway through. The blank being cut was from two-by-twelve (1½″ × 11½″) stock, and I figured the radius kind of close when marking, so the band saw cut off a half circle. I decided to leave it that way and see how it turned out. I liked the result.

Materials
- two-by-twelve × 16″ pine, or poplar
- three turned legs
- wood glue
- stain
- spray polyurethane

Tools
- measuring tape
- compass or trammel points and bar
- square
- band, scroll, or bayonet saw
- handsaw
- drill, ¾″ brad or Forstner bit
- router, ⅜″ round-over bit
- 100- and 150-grit sandpaper
- pad sander

Cut material to length at 16″, and mark 2″ in from edge of marked circle—set compass or points for a radius of 5¾″—for single leg hole (goes on end with curve). Mark in 2″ from each other corner (2″ in, 2″ down) and mark.

Drill holes, at a 10-degree angle (outside of angle to outside of stool: that is, the legs will splay, towards their bottoms, to the outside of the stool for stability).

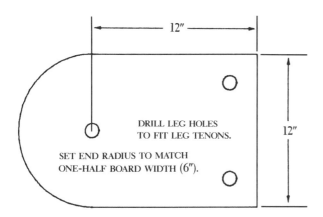

23-1. Three-legged stool pattern.

Cut half circle from stock, using band saw, scroll saw, or bayonet saw. Smooth edges, if needed, and then round over with router and bit.

Glue legs into holes, turn stool upside down, and place at least 30 lbs. on top of it for at least two hours.

Sand with 100-grit sandpaper, then 150-grit, and finish as desired, with stain and polyurethane, or with paint.

24 ◆ Quick Mug Racks

These mug racks start with oak mug pegs and oak boards to provide simple but practical home accessories.

Materials (for two)
- 52″ undrilled oak board
- six oak mug pegs
- woodworking glue
- tung oil
- No. 10 1½″ flathead wood screws

24-1. Quick mug racks.

Tools
- drill, ½″ Forstner bit
- measuring tape
- combination square

Measure the board to suit your location, with those shown being 16″ long. Space holes so each mug has at least 6″ to hang down below the peg. Drill the ½″ holes.

Drill holes for the No. 10 screws for application in your location.

Spread glue in holes and on tenons and place the pegs in holes. If the holes are exactly right, you'll need to apply a small amount of force. With no clamping or weighting really possible, give the glue at least 12 hours to set.

Sand, clean with a tack cloth, and finish with three coats of tung oil.

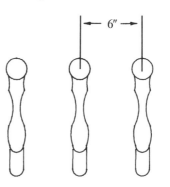

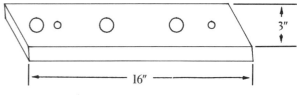

24-2. Drawing of mug rack.

25 ◆ Solid Cherry Framed Mirror

Frames are simple and useful projects, so I've included a few for use in various ways. The later (Chapter 4) and larger frame is designed to hold a wall mirror, while this smaller one may hold anything from a diploma to a drawing, and, of course, a small mirror.

Materials
- 8″ × 14″ bevelled flat glass mirror
- two ¾″ × 2″ × 10″ cherry
- two ¾″ × 2″ × 18″ cherry

Tools

- mitre box
- router, ⅜″ round-over bit, ¼″ rabbeting bit
- biscuit joiner
- four corner clamps
- soft hammer
- square
- measuring tape

Once the material is ripped and jointed to final size, the routing must be done.

I routed the rabbet first, making that ⅛″ deep by ¼″ wide. All router bits used were piloted types, so no edge guide was needed. After that, the round-overs were routed, in two passes.

The materials were then mitred at the corners, and cut to accept biscuits to give some extra joint strength over a flat mitre joint. Before mitring, check the actual mirror dimensions to make sure you're going to have a fit. I made a test assembly without glue, but with biscuits, and then disassembled the project, and came back with glue.

25-1. *Corner of mirror frame, glued and clamped.*

The glue was let dry overnight. Then the excess glue was scraped off, and the entire unit was sanded, front and back, progressing from 80- to 120- and 150-grit paper (that's as fine a paper as you need with cherry).

A tack rag took off the dust, and the entire assembly got its first coat of tung oil, wiped on in a moderate thickness. Next, the front was steel-wooled (0000). The tack rag was employed again, and the front of the frame got its second coat of tung oil, after being smoothed. The back of the frame was also coated, though not further smoothed. Third and fourth coats of tung oil were added over the next day or two.

Finally, flat plastic mounts were screwed in place behind the installed mirror, and a hanger mount was placed on the top center of the frame.

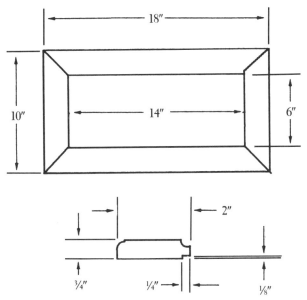

25-2. *Frame drawing.*

26 ◆ Walnut Wall Plate

This single-switch plate takes less than an hour to make. You may, in fact, make a good number in not much longer simply by making sure you've got ¼″ thick stock on hand, with grain that runs vertically (so it will run the 4″ dimension).

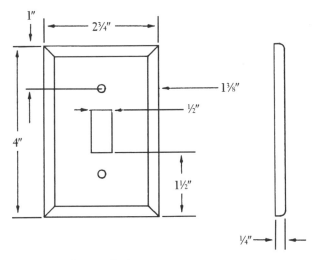

26-1. *Walnut wall plate.*

Materials

- 2¾″ × 4″ × ¼″ walnut (or preferred wood)
- polyurethane spray

Tools
- fine-toothed saw
- router, ¼″ or ³⁄₁₆″ round-over bit
- drill, ³⁄₁₆″ drill bit, and countersink
- ½″ chisel
- soft-faced hammer or mallet
- 150-grit sandpaper

Rip a strip 2¾″ wide, and cut vertically grained 4″ long pieces from that for the total number of wall plates desired.

Mark and drill the mounting holes, and drill corner holes for the ½″ × 1″ switch slot. Chisel out the switch slot, and smooth.

Round over the edges with a ⅛″ or ³⁄₁₆″ round-over router bit.

Sand with the 150-grit paper. Spray on several coats of polyurethane.

27 ◆ Walnut Double-Switch Wall Plate

This requires several more operations than the single-switch plate, but is no more difficult.

Materials
- 4½″ × 4″ × ¼″ walnut
- polyurethane spray

Tools
- fine-toothed saw
- router, ¼″ or ³⁄₁₆″ round-over bit
- drill, ³⁄₁₆″ drill bit, and countersink
- ½″ chisel
- soft-faced hammer or mallet
- 150-grit sandpaper

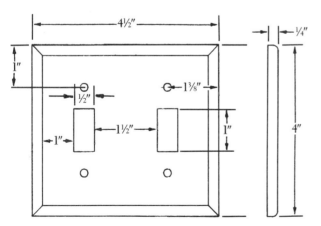

27-1. *Walnut double wall plate.*

The vertical grain still runs the 4″ direction, though that's not as important here as in the single plate. It does look better with grain running in the same direction, though.

Start by cutting the single piece, and marking hole positions. Drill all four holes, then drill holes at the corners of the two ½″ by 1″ slots. Chisel out the slots and smooth.

Round over the edges with the round-over bit and router.

Sand with 150-grit sandpaper. Spray on at least three coats of polyurethane.

28 ◆ Turned Walnut Candlestick

This is an easy turning job, drilled either to directly accept a candle or to accept a brass insert; I used the brass insert.

28-1. *Turned candlestick.*

Materials
- 4″ × 4″ × 6″ walnut turning block
- brass candle seat
- tung oil

28-2. *Several may be made from one turning blank.*

Tools
- lathe, gouge, skew
- 150-grit sandpaper
- drill or drill press, ⅝″ Forstner or brad point bit

Find centers at ends, and chuck the block in and mark off approximate divisions for the turning areas.

Start the rough turning, getting the end of the block round, and as large as possible. From there, cut down to the 1″ diameter at the opposite end, and turn to the pattern, using a caliper to measure.

When done, sand the bottom flat. I made several of these and had to trim each for length, which required a jig be made so the band saw wouldn't snatch the candlestick from one's hand.

The centering, or milling, vise set up for my drill press is exceptionally handy in such cases. The vise allows easy centering of such materials: I used ash strips to keep the vise jaws from marking the base of the candlestick.

Drill the hole for the candle, adjusting the drill bit size to fit the base of the candle that will be used.

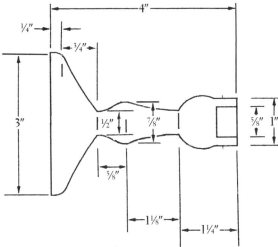

28-3. *Candlestick drawing.*

28-4. *Use shavings to polish the turned item.*

28-5. *Milling vise works well for aligning center hole for candle.*

29 ◆ Walnut Clock, Cardinal Face

Few projects are faster and easier than this one. I selected a rough-looking walnut blank, planed it smooth, and drilled for the clock motor.

Materials
- one-by-twelve × 12″ walnut (or other wood)
- clock motor, battery
- face
- satin polyurethane spray

Tools
- saw
- drill, 3″ drill bit
- 150-grit sandpaper
- measuring tape
- square

Start by identifying the corner in which you wish to locate the clock face. I liked the looks of the lower right location, which also went well with the knots up in one corner of my piece of wood.

Drill the 3″ hole far enough in to allow placing the 5″ diameter clock face well inside the board's edges. Sand lightly.

Mask off a 4½″ circle and then spray-finish the face and back of the board.

Install the clock motor on a hanger, and slip the face over the clock. Install the hands—carefully. Press the clock face (if it has self-stick adhesive) down firmly on the board. Install the battery, and set the time.

29-2. *Cardinal-faced board clock.*

30 ◆ Branch Spreader Series

Some trees, such as a batch of decorative and, soon, shade-providing Bradford pears I planted over the past couple years, have branches that grow without spreading properly from the main trunk. A fast cure is a branch spreader or two.

Materials
- 1″ × 4″ × 6″ wood
- 1″ × 4″ × 8″ wood
- 1″ × 4″ × 10″ wood

Tools
- scroll, band, or bayonet saw
- drill, 1½″ drill bit
- wood rasp

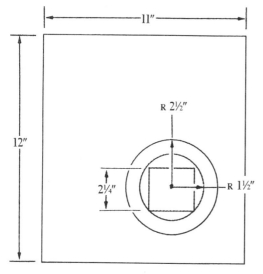

29-1. *Clock drawing.*

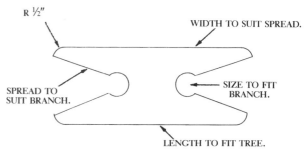

30-1. *Branch spreader drawing.*

Pieces are cut to length, as above. Mark in 2″ from each end and drill with the 1½″ bit, coming in from both sides to keep from splintering the wood.

Use the saw to cut into the hole sides, making a slight V shape towards those sides. Use a wood rasp to smooth and round corners.

Insert each spreader between trunk and branch, providing only gentle urging, not real force. As time passes, you will be able to push down a bit further, but don't give the spreader a really hard ram down into the crotch. Use the longer versions for larger branches.

31 ◆ One-Board Stool

This is based on a quick-shot seat for carpenters who need a place to have lunch. It is made of a single piece of two-by-twelve, sometimes with a chunk or two of two-by-six tossed in. Here, it's made of a chunk or two of two-by-twelve, with two-by-sixes as the base.

Materials
- **two-by-six × 96″**
- **two-by-twelve × 36″**
- **2½″ drive screws**

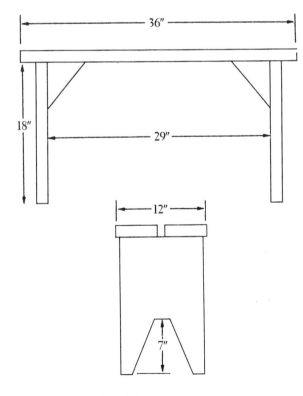

31-1. *One-board stool drawing.*

Tools
- **hand or circular saw**
- **mitre box**
- **screwdriver or clutched drill and driver bit**
- **drill, ⅛″ drill bit**
- **measuring tape**
- **square**

Begin by cutting two pieces of two-by-six to 36″ lengths. Next, cut two 18″ long pieces of two-by-twelve. Now, cut four pieces of two-by-six to a back length of 8″, with 45-degree angles on both ends to form a triangle.

Measure in 2″ from the edges of the long two-by-sixes and mark. Assemble the bench with drive screws, after drilling pilot holes. The two-by-twelve legs may first have a notch or arch cut at their lower ends to somewhat lighten the looks of the bench.

Use two drive screws for each two-by-six at the junction, and let each two-by-six hang over enough to provide a center opening of at least ¼″ between the two boards.

Come back and insert the 45-degree braces, drilling pilot holes and driving screws from both the two-by-twelve leg and the two-by-six top. There will be two braces per end, with each brace centered on its topside two-by-six.

32 ◆ Ten-Dowel Stool

This stool project is a delight for children, once it is built. And for the woodworker, it is truly "quick & easy."

32-1. *Exploded drawing of 10-dowel stool. (Courtesy of Dremel.)*

The only complexity in this stool is in the dowelling, and there the complexity is in the blind dowelling for the brace. This is made simple by using dowel points, instead of a dowelling jig. All the rest of the dowelling is open, and requires nothing more than accurate drilling, and sufficient glue. Remember to always drill dowel holes at least ⅛″ deeper than the dowel is long: the excess glue needs someplace to go.

It is best to use a drill press, or a portable drill guide, to align the holes accurately.

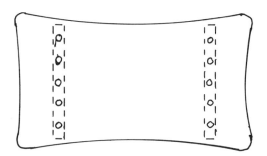

ALL HOLES ARE TO ACCOMMODATE 2″ × ¾″ DOWELS.

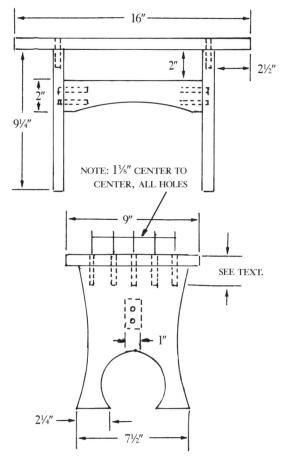

32-2. *Plan drawing of 10-dowel stool. (Courtesy of Dremel.)*

Materials
- 9″ × 16″ × ¾″ pine or fir (top)
- two 9¼″ × 7¼″ × 1¾″ (sides)
- 9½″ × 2¼″ × 1″ (brace)
- fourteen ⅜″ × 2″ dowels
- wood glue
- finishing material

Tools
- circular, table or handsaw
- scroll saw
- drill, ⅜″ brad point drill bit
- sander
- scraper
- ⅜″ dowel points (inserts)
- mallet
- four 24″ bar clamps

Cut all of the pieces to rectangular size first. At this time, mark all center points for dowelling, and use an awl or a center punch to prick the center points of dowel hole marks.

Transfer the curves onto their parts and make the needed cuts using a scroll saw, band saw, or jigsaw. Sand all edges, and then chamfer the edges lightly (do *not* chamfer edges that are to be glued).

Place glue in dowel holes and insert dowels with help from a mallet. Work from the top down, applying glue to the underside of the top where it will meet the top edges of the side boards, where glue is also applied. All surfaces to be joined, and all dowel holes, receive glue.

Clamp with bar clamps, and check for square. If you have a heavy workbench with a good, flat top, you might want to clamp the entire unit to the top of the workbench, as if it were in use. This will assure square in at least one direction.

When the glue has dried, cut the dowels off with a tenon or backsaw, leaving about ¹⁄₁₆″ above the surface of the wood. This is sanded flush. Cutting any closer is almost certain to gouge the wood.

33 ◆ Wall Mirror with Shelves

This mirror differs from the earlier wall mirror (Project 25) a great deal. It doesn't have a frame, as such, and the mirror is set between top and bottom shelves with a third shelf crossing the mirror in between.

Materials
- two ⅝″ × 5¼″ × 23″ (sides)
- ⅝″ × 2″ × 12¹⁄₁₆″ (top)

- ⅝″ × 2¾″ × 12¹⁄₁₆″ (shelf)
- ⅝″ × 4¼″ × 12¹⁄₁₆″ (bottom)
- ¼″ × 12″ × 20″ (back panel)
- two ⅜″ × ½″ × 11″ (back retainers)
- two ⅜″ × 11″ × 20½″ (side retainers)
- ⅛″ × ¾″ × 12¹⁄₁₆″ (mirror retainer)
- ⅛″ × 12″ × 20″ (mirror)
- fourteen No. 6 × 1½″ round-head brass screws
- nineteen ¾″ brass escutcheon pins

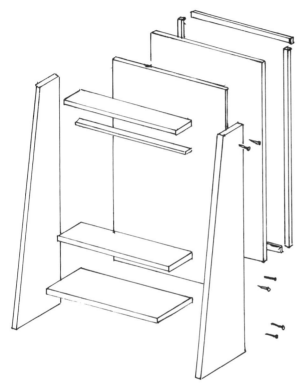

33-1.   *Wall mirror with shelf exploded drawing.
(Courtesy of Dremel.)*

Tools
- saw
- measuring tape
- square
- drill, and bit for No. 6 pilot holes
- 13 oz. hammer

Start by cutting all pieces to the listed sizes, and then cut the taper on the sides (taper from 5¼″ to 2½″ at the top). Sand pieces, slightly rounding the edges.

If you desire the pictured pattern, you can carve it by hand.

Attach top and bottom to sides, using screws. Attach mirror and back retainers to sides, top and bottom, in that order. Run a tiny bit of wood glue on the faces to

be joined and use the ¾″ brass escutcheon pins to do the joining. Keep the retainers flush at all edges.

Lay the partly assembled unit on its back, and drop in the back panel. Now, set the mirror in. Check for square.

Mark the third shelf location, and gently set that in place. Drill pilot holes, and attach the shelf. Place the mirror retainer against the top piece and the mirror, and attach with escutcheon pins (to the top).

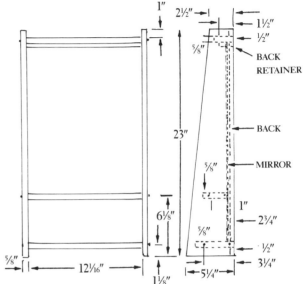

33-2.   *Plan drawing of wall mirror. (Courtesy of Dremel.)*

Finish. If you want to use a spray finish, stop assembly before the mirror goes in, and do the finish then.

34 ◆ Vanity Tray

This is a project that uses knockdown construction for glue-free assembly, using locking corner joints and a mirror held in place with a pin-held retainer.

The tray is designed to hold jewelry and perfume bottles, but might also be made without the mirror, facing the plywood bottom with a better grade of hardwood plywood to match the sides (to substitute, increase plywood thickness from ³⁄₁₆″ to ¼″, or even ⅜″).

Materials
- two ⅜″ × 2″ × 15″ cherry, walnut, or oak (long sides)
- two ⅜″ × 2″ × 9⅛″ (short sides)
- ⅜″ × 1½″ × 6¹³⁄₁₆″ (divider)
  Mirror supports:
- two ⁷⁄₁₆″ × ⅝″ × 12⅝″ (long sides)

- two $7/16'' \times 5/8'' \times 57/8''$ (short sides)
- $3/16'' \times 63/4'' \times 127/8''$ plywood (bottom)
- $1/8'' \times 63/4'' \times 127/8''$ mirror
- four $1/8'' \times 1''$ retaining pins
- twelve $5/8''$ brass escutcheon pins

Tools
- scroll or jigsaw
- handsaw
- sander
- measuring tape
- square
- $1/2''$ chisel
- light 24'' bar clamps
- scribe
- 13 oz. hammer

Start by cutting all materials to the correct sizes. Based on the mirror dimensions, lay out locking joint locations, using the scribe and the square. Cut angled ends on sides and ends after laying out locking joints. Sand down any rough edges.

You may wish to run a small dowel ($1/8'' \times 11/2''$) into the ends between the locking joints and those ends; if you do, drill up from the bottom to hide the dowel. The dowel will add considerably to strength at a point that is badly weakened by notching for the locking joint.

Cut the notches with a scroll saw or a fine-toothed coping saw. Cut only along the long lines, and use a sharp chisel to cut at the short line. Relieve the joint area with the chisel, paring a thin taper towards the notch. Check-fit each of the joints as they are cut, taking great

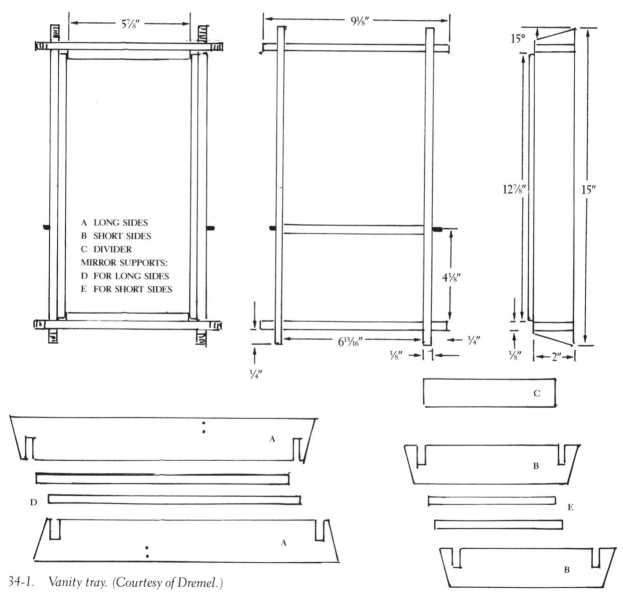

34-1.   Vanity tray. (Courtesy of Dremel.)

care not to open the joint, or sand down the side, too much. A snug, firm fit is best, though *too* tight a fit splits the wood.

Cut and insert the mirror supports, rubbing a bit of glue on the supports after drilling pilot holes for the pins (use a pin in a drill to get the holes, and make the holes shorter than the pin to be used). Install the mirror supports, and then check for square and install the bottom. Insert the mirror and check again for square.

Check the divider fit, and drill ⅛″ holes about 1″ deep in the ends of the divider, and through the sides of the tray. Retaining pins are cut from ⅛″ dowel stock. Trial-fit the divider and the pins.

Sand and finish and reassemble, after staining the retaining pins as dark a color as possible.

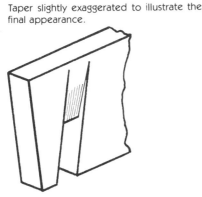

First cut side marking lines with chisel - then pare a thin taper towards the notch.

34-2. *Locking end paring. (Courtesy of Dremel.)*

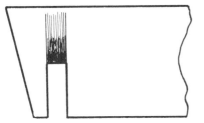

Taper slightly exaggerated to illustrate the final appearance.

34-3. *Taper. (Courtesy of Dremel.)*

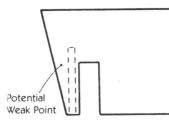

Potential Weak Point

34-4. *Dowels to strengthen wood. (Courtesy of Dremel.)*

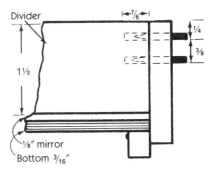

34-5. *Retaining pins. (Courtesy of Dremel.)*

35 ♦ Belt and Tie Bar

This project is complex only in the need for drilling a good number of holes with moderate precision. It is then screwed to a wall, and all ties and belts in one's closet and other areas may be arranged neatly.

35-1. *Belt and tie bar.*

Materials
- 28″ × 3″ × 1″ oak
- thirty-four miniature shaker pegs
- seven mini-coat hooks
- wood glue
- stain
- spray polyurethane

Tools
- saw
- router, cove bit
- drill, ⅛″, ¼″ brad point bit
- mallet
- toothpicks
- 1½″ counterbore
- 100- and 150-grit sandpaper
- pad sander

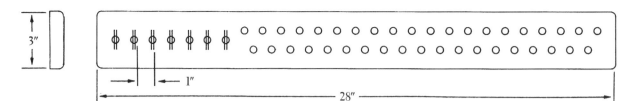

35-2.   Belt and tie bar drawing.

Start by cutting the bar to size. Then mark the end holes for wall attachment 1″ in from ends, and centered. Mark a midline across the entire board, and then drill mounting holes with the counterbore.

Mark seven center points starting 1¾″ in from the left side, spacing them 1½″ apart. Drill ⅛″ × ½″ deep pilot holes for the mini-coat hooks.

Mark two rows, each 1″ down from an edge, for the Shaker pegs: start 1″ in from the right edge, on the bottom row, and 1½″ in on the top row. Space marks 1″ on center on both rows. Drill, using the ¼″ brad point bit, holes for peg tenons that are ⅜″ deep.

Rout edges with the cove bit once all holes are drilled. Rout ends first, then long edges with the grain, which cleans up any tearing of end grain. If you use a steel bit, make two passes to get the cove. A carbide tip allows the job to be done in a single pass. Sand well.

Carefully place glue in one row of holes, using a toothpick, and wipe a light coat of glue around the tenons on 17 pegs. Place those, tapping into place with a mallet. Do the same with the second row.

Dry-wipe any spilled glue. Make sure of glue clean-up, and sand with the 150 grit sandpaper, hand-held.

Stain, and, after six hours, spray on the first coat of polyurethane. After six to eight more hours, spray on another coat, and finish with a third four to six hours later.

Turn in the screw-based mini-coat hooks, and the tie bar is ready for hanging.

36 ✦ Door-Back Clothing Bar

This teak-stained oak clothing bar provides a "quick & easy" project that also makes a good gift. It also works quite well in places other than on the back of a bedroom door, though that's where mine ended up, catching pajamas, robes, and such.

Materials
- 3½″ × 20″ × 1″ white oak bar
- five oak Shaker pegs
- wood glue
- white oak stain
- antique flat polyurethane

Tools
- saw
- router, cove, or round-over bit
- drill, ½″ brad point bit
- mallet
- measuring tape
- square
- sander
- 100- and 150-grit sandpaper

Start by cutting the oak to size. Mark a midline, at 1¾″, and mark for the first two ½″ holes each 1½″ in from an end. Mark 3½″ over from each of those, to the inside, and mark for the next pegs. Mark the next hole at board's center (10″ from the short edge). Drill the holes ⅝″ deep to accept the tenons of the pegs.

Mark the hanging screw holes in 3″ from each short edge, on the centerline, and drill, going deep enough to allow a rounded oak plug to be tapped into place after the bar is hung.

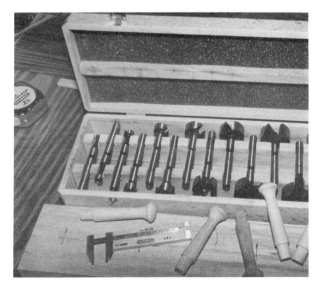

36-1.   Mark as shown and drill tenon holes with brad point or Forstner bit.

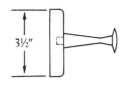

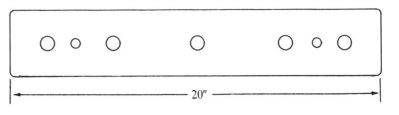

36-2. *Clothing bar drawing.*

Sand with 100- and 150-grit sandpaper, clean with a cloth. Spread wood glue on the hole bottoms and sides, and on the peg tenons. Do not spread glue excessively, but make sure coverage is adequate. Tap the pegs into the holes.

36-3. *Back-of-door clothing bar.*

36-4. *Rout cove after drilling, or, at least, after marking for drilling.*

After two hours' drying for the glue, check for glue spills, and scrape any found. Sand lightly. Clean with a tack cloth, and stain. Brush on the flat finish.

37 ◆ Cherry-and-Maple Cutting Board

This project came to mind from my collection scraps around the shop.

Materials
- fifteen 18″ × 1½″ × ¾″ cherry and maple
- wood glue
- salad bowl finish

37-1. *Cherry and maple cutting board.*

3/4"

11¼"

18"

37-2. *Cutting board drawing.*

Tools
- saw
- measuring tape
- square
- plane
- belt sander, 120-grit belt
- three 18" bar clamps

This job is truly simple. Cut material to size, and determine the layout of strips for the most pleasing appearance. Check for fit inside clamps. Lay clamps out so they will be flat on bench top. Strips can rest on a clamp bar, which makes for a reasonably even glued surface.

Lay strips on clamps and apply glue, tipping each strip into place as glue is applied. Tighten clamps when done, and dry-wipe squeeze-out after that.

When clamping is done (at least two hours, preferably overnight), scrape glue off the surface and sand smooth. I scraped mine and then ran it through a planer, after which I used a 10" compound mitre saw to square the ends at 18".

Originally, I'd expected to cut a meat juice groove and a hanging hole in the board, but once I put a couple of coats of salad bowl finish on, I decided to leave well enough alone. Sometimes things are better that way.

38 ♦ Redwood Butcher Block Bench

This is a porch, deck, patio or yard use project, but it's so easy I decided to include it in this chapter. All material is two-by-four stock redwood, surfaced. Use heart redwood lumber for legs if they're going to touch the ground, and construction common redwood for the bench. Lengths needed vary with the size of bench made.

38-1. *Redwood bench, butcher-block style. (Courtesy of the California Redwood Association.)*

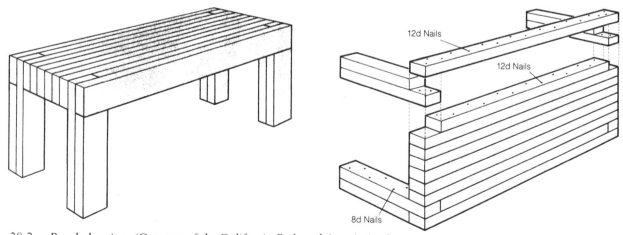

38-2. *Bench drawing. (Courtesy of the California Redwood Association.)*

Materials
- 4′ size: two 6′, five 8′ lengths
- 6′ size: twelve 6′ lengths
- 8′ size: ten 8′, two 6′ lengths
- 10′ size: ten 10′, two 6′ lengths
- 8d and 12d galvanized nails

Tools
- hammer
- saw, mitre box
- plane or sander

Make four legs out of the two-by-fours, cutting four to 18″ lengths and four to 14½″ lengths (this second measurement is critical, so check the *actual* width of your two-by-fours to subtract from the 18″ length). Nail in pairs, a long and a short, with 8d nails, six nails to a leg.

Trim two pieces of the 10 needed for the seat to allow for insertion of the legs. Again, measure to get the actual trimming allowance, which should be about 7″, total, per length. Lay one full-length two-by-four on the ground, and nail legs at each end, with 8d nails. Build up the nail-laminate from there, with nails in a zigzag pattern, every 6″. Nail the second two-by-four to the first with 8d nails, and after that use 12d nails. The ninth two-by-four will again be a short one, filled out at the ends with a pair of legs. Continue with 12d nails. When the bench is finished, flip it over and do the first two-by-four with 12d nails.

If necessary, plane or sand the seat to even its surface. No finish is needed, but you may want to add a water repellent—test this on a small piece of scrap first to make sure the chemicals don't darken the redwood.

39 ◆ Redwood Four-by-Four Planter

This planter is sizable, but reasonable in weight when empty, as well as being very attractive. Use construction heart redwood whenever ground contact is likely. Otherwise, construction common is fine.

39-1. *Redwood four-by-four planter. (Courtesy of the California Redwood Association.)*

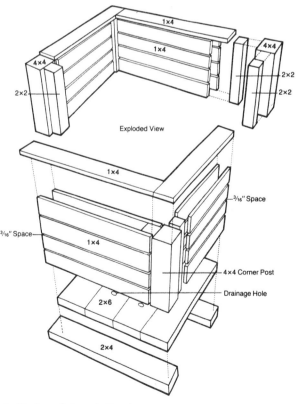

39-2. *Redwood planter drawing. (Courtesy of the California Redwood Association.)*

Materials
- four four-by-four × 15″ (heart)
- sixteen one-by-four × 22½″ (heart)
- four two-by-six × 22½″ (heart)
- two two-by-four × 24½″ (heart)
- sixteen one-by-four × 22½″
- four one-by-four × 26½″
- eight two-by-two × 15″
- 12d galvanized nails
- 6d galvanized nails

Tools
- circular saw
- mitre box
- square
- measuring tape
- hammer

Start by cutting lumber to size, making sure ends are square. Nail the two-by-twos to adjacent faces of each four-by-four post with 12d nails. Leave room for the one-by-fours to fit flush with outer face of the four-by-fours. Attach one-by-four boards to posts with 6d nails, two at each end. Space one-by-fours evenly along the post, and flush with bottom and outer face. Use construction heart for interior walls.

Complete two walls, inside and out, to form an L. Construct the next two walls, and lay the project on its side as you complete the nailing of the box.

To make the base, turn the box upside down, and place two-by-fours on opposite sides, an inch in from each edge. Use two 12d nails at each end to attach the two-by-fours to the four-by-four posts. Turn the box upright, and lay all four two-by-six pieces in to form the box bottom.

Top trim is butt-jointed one-by-fours flush with the planter's outside edge. Use two 6d nails at each board end, one end into the four-by-four and one end into the two-by-two.

It's best to line the planter with polyethylene, which needs drain holes cut into it. The two-by-sixes will last longer if there are a few ½″ holes drilled into them.

40 ♦ Weather Bar

Checking the weather in advance of the evening news is always an interesting thing to do. This set of weather instruments has brass rings for mounting, instead of the instruments being mounted in holes. The whole thing takes very little time.

Materials
- 5″ × 18″ ash board
- thermometer
- hygrometer
- barometer
- clock
- four mounting rings
- tung oil
- twelve ½″ × ⅛″ escutcheon pins
- saw-tooth hanger
- 120-grit sandpaper

Cut the ash board to length, and mark for locations of the instruments. The ash I used was some bought locally and dried. (So my project really required a table saw for ripping, a planer for initial smoothing and sizing to ¾″ thickness, and a jointer for edging, as well as the 10 months or so for drying.) The 3″ mounting rings make assembly simple: nail them in position, and the instruments are a push-fit into the rings. Make the board long enough so you can position the rings along the midline at least 1″ apart at their edges.

40-1. *Rings mounted.*

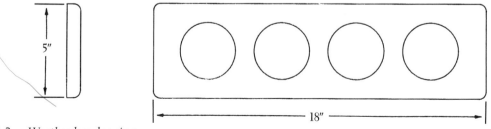

40-2. *Weather bar drawing.*

Tools
- router, round-over bit
- saw
- hammer
- nail set
- finishing sander

40-3.   *Weather bar.*

Place a saw-toothed hanger in the center of the back top edge. I finished, before adding the hardware and instruments, with three coats of tung oil, put on with an old T-shirt.

41 ◆ Splined Cherry Picture Frame

This frame is made of local cherry, and splined with the same wood. The splines are cut so the grain runs long ways.

Materials
- two 16″ × 1¼″ × 1″ cherry
- two 14″ × 1¼″ × 1″ cherry
- four 2″ × 1″ × ⅛″ cherry splines
- wood glue
- saw-tooth hanger
- tung oil
- 120-grit sandpaper

Tools
- table saw
- mitre saw
- router, ⅜″ round-over bit and rabbeting bit
- hammer

The cherry is cut to size and shaped with passes on both sides by the router, after a ⅜″ × ⅜″ rabbet is cut. The rabbet needs to be deep enough to hold the glass (⅛″), matting, picture, and backer (⅛″) as well as push-points—thus ⅜″ deep. If the matting is very thick, you may need to increase the depth of the rabbet to ½″. That will take two passes with most router bits.

Once shaping and mitring is done, the table saw is set to depth and the spline cut is made. Depth is half the thickness of the stock, with the spline set about one-third of the way down from the front top of the frame.

Splines are glued in, and the frame is allowed to dry, after being squared up. Excess spline is first cut off, and then sanded down, after which the tung oil is applied.

When the tung oil is dry, fit the glass to the front, and apply matting, picture, and backer.

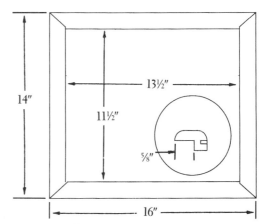

41-1.   *Frame drawing.*

41-2.   *Check spline fit before glue-up.*

4 · General Projects

These projects cover a wide area, and are generally a bit more complex than those in the preceding chapter. They may take a little longer to do, but may not need many more materials or tools.

42 ♦ Knock-Together Scrap-Wood Tool Stand

This is a "quick & easy" tool stand I use to fit a portable table saw. It went together out of scraps in the shop—which accounts for all the different wood. There's no reason on earth to use pressure-treated four-by-four uprights, as you may see I did, unless you happen to have four equal-size uprights handy. In fact, two-by-four is heavy enough.

42-1. *Scrap wood tool stand, with table saw mounted.*

Materials
- four four-by-four × 20″ Southern pine
- four two-by-four × 24″ pine
- four two-by-four × 22″ pine
- 22″ × 24″ × ¾″ B-C plywood
- 22″ × 24″ × ¼″ OSB or waferboard
- 12d common nails
- 4d and 6d nails
- wood glue

Tools
- circular or table saw
- square
- measuring tape
- hammer

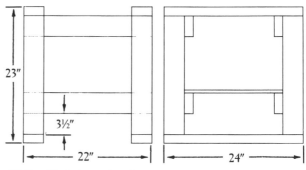

42-2. *Tool stand drawing.*

Start by cutting pieces to length. Make two leg sets by gluing and nailing the 24″ two-by-fours to tops and bottoms of the four-by-fours. Make sure the units are square. Now, measure up 3½″ on front and back lower edges of each set, and nail and glue the 22″ two-by-fours there and just under the top two-by-fours. The result is a sturdy box.

You now want to add the ¼″ sawdust shield just under the top of the top two-by-fours, using 4d nails to fasten it there. Notch the shelf corners and install that with 6d finishing nails and glue.

42-3. *Scrap wood tool stand.*

Both width and depth are easily varied to allow simple mounting of almost any small table saw; but, if there is a mounting problem, simply don't add the saw-dust shield, and do add a 24″ square ¾″ plywood top, to which you can mount anything.

The height can also be varied to suit different tools and workers.

43 ◆ Desk Organizer

This little organizer gets bills and letters up off the flat surface of your desk, and provides a small box for small items such as stamps, rubber bands, and paper clips. A half-size unit might also be used for supporting floppy disks. Select base wood for matching plywood availability—white birch, white oak, cherry, etc.

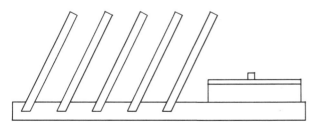

43-1. *Desktop organizer.*

Materials
- 1″ × 10⁵⁄₃₂″ × 18¼″ (base, full 1″ thick)
- five ³⁄₈″ × 5½″ × 10⅛″ (dividers)
- 145″ veneer tape (dividers and lid edge strips)
- two ⁷⁄₁₆″ × 1″ × 8¾″ (box long sides)
- two ⁷⁄₁₆″ × 1″ × 4⅞″ (short sides)
- ³⁄₈″ × 5⅛″ × 10″ (lid)
- two ¼″ × 3¹³⁄₁₆″ × 1″ (lid-securing strips)
- ⁷⁄₁₆″ × ⅝″ × 5⅝″ (lid handle)
- twelve 1¼″ × ⅛″ dowels
- No. 6 × 1½″ panhead sheet-metal screws
- four ³⁄₈″ diameter felt pads
- nine ½″ brass escutcheon pins
- wood glue

Tools
- saw
- measuring tape
- try square
- protractor
- drill, ⅛″ bit
- router or rotary tool, ¼″ straight router bit
- light bar clamps

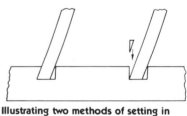

Illustrating two methods of setting in dividers.

43-2. *Filling in with wedges. (Courtesy of Dremel.)*

Start by sizing all pieces. Getting the solid woods to recommended thicknesses is one of the hardest parts, along with cutting the slots.

Make the box by butt-gluing the corners with the long sides placed *inside* the short sides. Clamp lightly, after squaring up. Drill ⅛″ holes to accept the dowels and insert these before the glue totally dries. Coat the dowels with glue and insert. Scrape or sand off excess glue after it dries. Trim off excess dowel stock and sand the box to its final finish readiness.

Iron-on the heat-sensitive strips for the box lid and divider edges. Sand off any lip overhang.

If you use a full-size router with the slots, use a 14-degree ½″ dovetail bit to cut the slots. Otherwise, cut with a straight bit, to ½″ wide by ⅜″ deep. Make a bevel cut on the bottom edges of the dividers, and the fit will

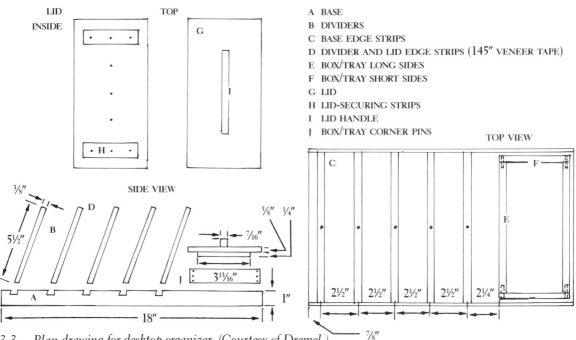

A	BASE
B	DIVIDERS
C	BASE EDGE STRIPS
D	DIVIDER AND LID EDGE STRIPS (145″ VENEER TAPE)
E	BOX/TRAY LONG SIDES
F	BOX/TRAY SHORT SIDES
G	LID
H	LID-SECURING STRIPS
I	LID HANDLE
J	BOX/TRAY CORNER PINS

43-3. *Plan drawing for desktop organizer. (Courtesy of Dremel.)*

be decent; make the bevel cut at 20 degrees, using a protractor to set and check the saw and the final cut.

Using a ½″ dovetail bit, set to ⁵⁄₁₆″ deep, make the slots. Then enlarge the *back* side of the opening to ⁷⁄₁₆″ at the top (the ½″ bit measurement is at the bit bottom). Make slight wedges and fit those into the front part of each slot, ahead of the dividers, and the appearance will be good. Insert and glue the dividers, after preparing the wedges.

Use an oversize drill bit to go through the base parallel to the dividers, but not into them. Countersink these holes. Drill into the dividers with an undersize bit to make pilot holes. Coat the insides of the dadoes with glue, insert the dividers, and drive in the screws.

Mark the box location, and drill countersunk holes in the base, and pilot holes in the box sides. After carefully positioning the box on the base, and over the countersunk holes, screw the base to the box with one screw

per short side. Place glue on the bottom edges of short side lengths and draw them up tight with the screws.

Assemble the lid, as shown. Make sure to use pilot holes for all lid parts, and attach with glue, as well as the brass pins.

Finish is up to you, but for a project such as this, after sanding through a 150 grit paper, I would suggest a spray-on polyurethane, in a satin finish. Apply an adhesive felt pad to each corner after the finish dries.

44 ♦ Wall Mirror Frame

This frame is made of cherry, and is designed to fit a 14″ × 54″ bevelled glass mirror. It's simple construction, and goes together in fairly short order, once the router work is done.

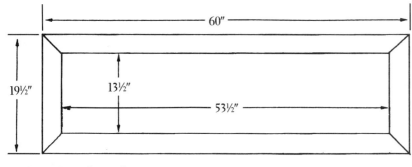

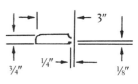

44-1. *Mirror frame drawing.*

Materials

- two ¾″ × 3″ × 60″ cherry (optional)
- two ¾″ × 3″ × 20″ cherry
- 14″ × 54″ bevelled float glass mirror
- four joiner biscuits
- wood glue
- tung oil
- four brass mending plates, with screws
- six mirror mounts
- six ½″ self-stick felt dots

Tools

- biscuit joiner
- mitre box
- router, ⅜″ round-over, ¼″ rabbetting, and ⅜″ cove router bits
- four corner clamps
- 100 and 150 grit sandpaper
- pad sander

Start by making sure all wood is as described, though you need not use cherry. Round over the outside edges of the wood, and then rout the ¼″ × ⅛″ deep rabbet into which the mirror will fit. The final routing is the inside edge with its cove cut.

Mitre all corners, assemble dry, and mark the corners for cutting the slots for the plates. Cut the slots, and assemble, dry, to test-fit with the biscuits.

Set up corner clamps within one turn of being ready, and then glue the unit, two corners at a time. Doing only two corners allows squaring and adjustment before locking the clamps. Allow to dry at least 12 hours, then scrape off excess glue at corners.

Sand with 100 grit sandpaper, and then 150 grit. Wipe on tung oil, following the manufacturer's directions.

Install the mirror, using the six mirror-installation buttons turned upside down, clamping down on the felt buttons stuck under the clamp buttons, on the mirror back.

Place the four straight sections of brass mending plates equidistant down from the top and up from the bottom, with two screws into each plate and the mirror frame. The plates are then used, from the front, to let you screw into the back of the door, or wall, on which the mirror is being mounted.

44-2. Wall mirror.

44-3. Brass mending plates, mirror holders, and felt buttons keep the mirror in the frame and the frame on the wall or door.

45 ♦ Equipment Box

This is a general-use box of pine. Boards are glued up and cut to width, and the dovetails, if used, are cut with a jig. All of the wide material is glued up from two one-by-six and one one-by-eight pieces and cut to exact size. Two easier-to-make designs of this equipment box follow in Project 46 and Project 47. There the simplification that requires fewer tools is to eliminate the dovetail joints.

Materials
- two 18″ × 18″ × 1″ pine
- three 18″ × 30″ × 1″ pine
- 18″ × 30″ × ⅜″ plywood
- 16½″ × 28½″ × ¼″ plywood
- three 2″ × 28½″ × 1″ pine
- three 2″ × 15″ × 1″ pine
- 30″ × 1½″ piano hinge and hasp
- wood glue

Tools
- router
- dovetail jig, with bits
- two C-clamps
- mallet
- four 24″ bar clamps
- four 36″ bar clamps
- cabinet screwdriver
- measuring tape
- square
- table saw
- 1″ masking tape
- ⅛″ shims
- belt sander, 100 grit belt
- pad sander, 100, 150, 180 grit sandpaper
- stain or paint
- clear finish (if stain is used)

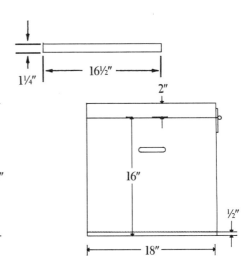

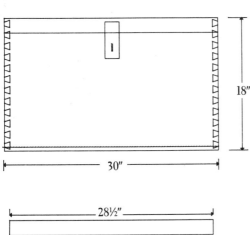

45-1.   *Equipment box drawing.*

Start by gluing wood up as indicated, to get the above general sizes. Allow glue to dry overnight. Sand flat, after scraping off excess glue.

Lay out parts and determine top, bottom, etc. Cut ⅜″ × ⅜″ rabbet in tops of sides, back, and front. Cut same size rabbet in top, all four sides. Cut a ⅜″ × ⅜″ deep rabbet along each bottom edge (so it will face the inside). Final-cut the ⅜″ plywood to fit the bottom. Check for fit and make any needed adjustments before final-cutting of side joints.

Cut dovetails, if they're being used, and dry-assemble sides, front, and back. If fit is fine, assemble with glue and square up (check each corner with a square, or measure diagonals to see that they match). Assemble the box whole, top and all.

Cut the top loose, 2″ down from top of the box, on the table saw. Start by taping the line to be cut, with masking tape. Set the rip fence, and assemble some ⅛″ shims. Start the cut to remove the top along one long side. Shim and move to the next long side. Shim close to the next cut, and cut one end loose. Shim, turn, and cut the final end loose. Cutting the top in this manner assures a near-perfect fit.

Remove masking tape, and install tray supports with their tops 3″ below the lip of the box bottom. Assemble the tray of ¼″ plywood (set into ⅜″ × ¼″ rabbets in the bottoms of the ends and sides of the tray) so its final dimension is ¼″ less in each direction than is the inside of the constructed box.

Sand box, and stain or paint as desired. Install piano hinge, and hasp.

46 ♦ Finger-Jointed Equipment Box

Instead of working in dovetail joints with a dovetail jig, use a finger-joint jig to make ½″ finger joints in the outside of the box. Otherwise, tool needs and general materials needs are similar to or the same as for Project 45. If you decide to carry through with the finger joints, adjust the top height so that the cut line on the table saw intersects one of the joints at a point that will leave at least three-quarters of a joint on the bottom part of the box.

47 ♦ Lap-Jointed Equipment Box

The easiest way of making the basic box (Project 45) is to use end lap joints. There are ⅜″ × ⅜″ rabbets cut into opposing sides and ends to give a fit that exposes only ⅜″ of end grain. You may, if you wish, go ahead and work that rabbet depth down as much as ⅝″, exposing only ⅛″ of end grain, but the joint will not be quite as strong.

This version requires no fancy jigs, and, in fact, no extra tools because you will already have a ⅜″ rabbetting bit on hand for earlier uses.

As with any variant, make sure all parts fit before starting to glue up, and make sure the rabbets are all cut in properly related ways so that the joints do lap.

48 ♦ Tall Slanted Shelves

Some years ago, I had, for one reason or another, actually lost all of my shelving. I had to have some shelves, and so, as a result, I adapted ideas from all kinds of things, to produce a slanted shelf system that really works quite well. The shelves are all made of waferboard, with the backer board a full 48″ wide, clipped off to fit under ceilings.

48-1. *Tall slanted shelves.*

Materials
- three 4′ × 8′ sheets, ¾″ waferboard
- 8d finishing nails
- 48″ × ¾″ × 3½″ pine
- stain or paint
- final coat, if needed

Tools
- circular saw
- spring clamps
- measuring tape
- framing square
- combination square
- bayonet saw
- chalk line
- hammer

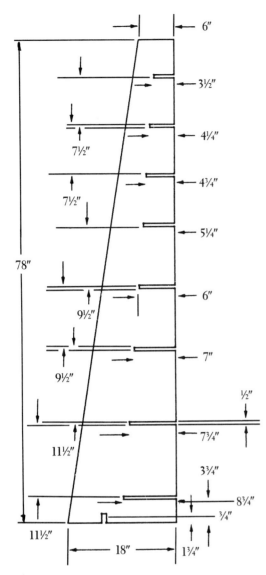

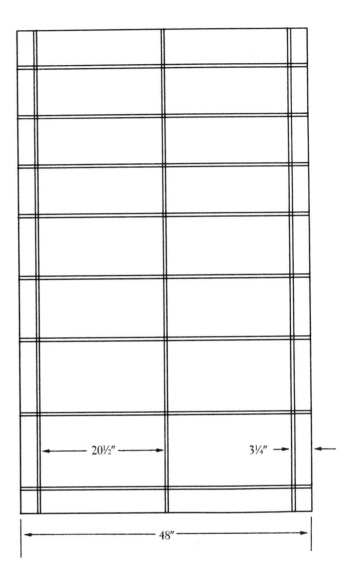

48-2. *Slant shelf drawing.*

Start by cutting the uprights, making sure they'll be spaced about 21″ to 22″ on center (actual dimensions are less important than keeping them the same for each shelf built). For my 78″ tall uprights, I used a top depth of 6″ expanding to a bottom of 18″. It's thus easy to cut three of these from a single sheet of waferboard.

Shelves are cut a full 48″ wide.

Space the cuts in the uprights for the shelves as shown. The easiest way to make sure all spacing is the same across three, or four, uprights is to clamp the uprights together, mark the top one, and cut them all at one time. This is also the fastest way both to mark and to cut the units.

Decide where the shelves are to fit, and cut to depth. I do mine with the top, narrow shelf clamped atop all the

others, making a cut to the limits of the top shelf. That is then removed and the cuts extended ½″—or ¾″ or 1″—as demanded by the plan for each succeeding shelf, as the uppermost unit is cut and removed. Use the bayonet saw to remove the stock in the slots.

Cut the baseboard brace (the one-by-four pine) in the same manner, to the dimensions shown. Lay the uprights down, and insert the slotted shelves. This is much easier with a helper, but once top and bottom shelves are on, all goes quickly.

Insert the baseboard brace, and square up the framework. Nail at junctions, into the shelves. You may use wood or construction glue if you wish at the same points. Once everything is squared, mark the backboard sizes, and cut to fit. Place that with 6d finishing nails, spaced at 8″ intervals.

49 ♦ Low Slanted Shelves

Not too long after the above shelf was built, I needed a lower unit for basement storage.

The simplicity of the change is remarkable. Take dimensions to a 48″ height and retain all sizes underneath, but expand the width to 96″. Make four uprights—five if you expect to be storing many heavy items. Shelves, of course, become 96″ wide, as does the baseboard brace.

49-1. Wide slanted shelf.

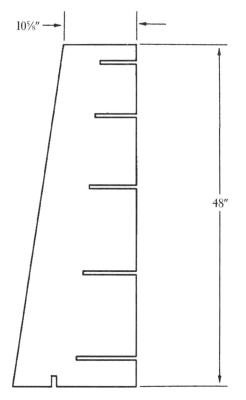

49-2. Wide shelf drawing.

If you need a size other than 48″ high, simply pick off those dimensions and go to it. You can either taper from 18″ down to 6″ really quick, or, as in the 48″ high unit, taper to the between size, which is 10⅝″ at 4′. Actually, I also moved the top shelf down 2″ on that version.

Any of the shelves will prove virtually tip-proof. I later made some ½″ stock versions that hold a lot of books with no problems. But the ½″ thickness for shelves is really not adequate for all uses.

50 ♦ Easy End Table

If you have a jointer, this table is super-easy. If not, it's a bit more difficult, but not really hard to make.

Materials
• four 1½″ × 1½″ × 16¼″ pine or fir
• two 1″ × 5″ × 12½″ pine or fir
• two 1″ × 5″ × 24″ pine or fir
• four 1″ × 5″ × 30″ pine or fir
• two 1″ × 1″ × 28″ pine or fir
• eight ⅜″ × 2½″ dowels
• eight ⅜″ flat-top dowel plugs
• six No. 10 × 1½″ round-head wood screws
• 2″ masking tape
• stain, or paint
• clear coating, if needed

Tools
• jointer or hand plane
• circular or table saw
• angle jig for circular saw if no jointer or hand plane
• jigsaw, band or scroll saw
• drill, ⅜″, 5⁄32″ bits
• measuring tape
• square
• pad sander, 100- and 150-grit sandpaper
• 24″ bar or pipe clamps, three or four
• two 36″ bar clamps

Start by cutting all pieces to size, and gluing up the top boards to form a flat board 17½″ wide by 29″ long. Allow glue to dry thoroughly, then scrape off excess glue and sand flat.

Mask the legs at the 4″ mark down from the top. **Caution:** tape back the safety guard on your jointer—which means all moves *must* be made very carefully, and you MUST use a push pad—and start successive cuts on the legs, all four sides, at that point. Reduce each side of each leg by ⅛″ at the bottom tip.

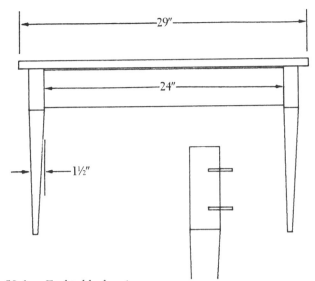

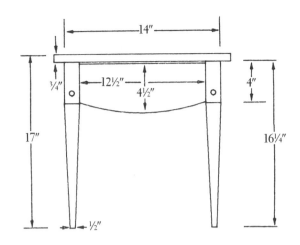

50-1. *End table drawing.*

Mark the curve on the ends and cut with jigsaw, band saw or scroll saw. Make the mark by driving a nail just off the edge of bottom center and arching a ripped 1/16″ thick section of wood from the 4″ mark to that nail and around to the 4″ mark (at board ends for the 4″ marks). Cut the curves.

Assemble the ends using clamps. Drill, glue, and dowel after assembly is tight in the clamps. Repeat the process for the sides, using 36″ bar clamps.

Glue the one-by-one strips on the inside tops of the sides.

Check everything for square, and settle the tabletop in place. Mark for screws from underneath, up through the one-by-one blocks. Drill with the 5/32″ bit, and assemble with wood screws.

Sand carefully with 100 and 150 grit sandpaper, and then stain. Coat with polyurethane after staining. If the project is painted, don't bother with 150 grit sandpaper.

51 ◆ Bookcase

We needed a small bookcase for a small spot, and there was barely any time left in the weekend, so I designed and built the enclosed unit in about three hours. I like to refer to this as my "Lazy Person's Bookcase Project," because it all went so quickly. The finish added another hour of work needing to be done the second day. This bookcase is simple, sturdy, and reasonably attractive, depending on your choice of wood.

51-1. *Bookcase.*

Materials

- two one-by-ten × 36″ pine or fir (sides)
- four one-by-ten × 23″ pine or fir (top, bottom, shelves)
- 48″ × 1″ × 3″ pine or fir (top trim)
- 48″ × 1″ × 4″ pine or fir (base trim)
- 24″ × 32¼″ × ¼″ tempered hardboard, lauan, or waferwood (backboard)
- 6d finishing nails
- 4d finishing nails
- four 36″ shelf standards
- eight shelf clips
- stain
- polyurethane finish

Tools

- square
- measuring tape
- mitre box with at least 3½″ *upright* capacity
- handsaw or circular saw
- router, ⅜″ rabbetting, ⅜″ cove, ¾″ straight bits
- router edge guide
- hammer
- nail set
- four 36″ bar clamps
- wood glue
- 100- and 150-grit sandpaper
- pad sander

Cut all pieces to size, remembering that the one-inch thickness is nominal (thus is really about ¾″), as is the four-inch base width, which is really about 3½″. The top trim is ripped from 2½″ to 2″ wide. Both have one edge routed in a cove. Rout the ⅜″ wide by ¼″ deep rabbet on the inside back edges of all materials, and trim

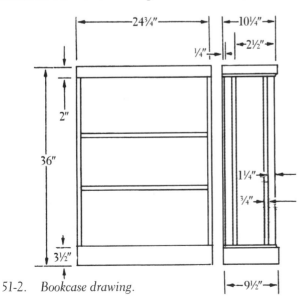

51-2. *Bookcase drawing.*

¼″ off each movable shelf's depth (to allow for backboard depth). Rout a ¾″ groove 1½″ in from the inside front of both boards, and another 2″ in from the inside back (these accept the shelf standards, and should be about ¼″ deep). Install shelf standards in their grooves.

Butt-join the top and sides and the bottom and sides, keeping the bottom so its top edge is exactly 3½″ from the bottom of the side boards. Square, glue, and nail with three or four 6d finishing nails at each junction. Clamp for a couple of hours.

Mitre corners on the top and bottom trim and install with glue and 6d nails. Scrape off excess glue after removing the clamps. Sand with both grit sandpapers, and wipe down good, preferably with a tack cloth. Stain. After that dries, lay on at least two coats of polyurethane. Set the shelves in place and fill.

52 ◆ Sit-Up Board

Not all of us can get to the gym every time we wish. Having exercise equipment around when we can't get out is a large help. *Do not start any exercise program without consulting your doctor—and avoid any abdominal exercises if you have back problems.*

This slant board is heavy-duty, and provides a three-stop range over 30″.

Materials

- two ¾″ × 72″ × 16½″ plywood
- two ¾″ × 24″ × 30″ plywood (sides)
- ¾″ × 20″ × 24″ (base plate)
- 1¼″ hardwood dowel, 24″
- four 3″ corner angles
- two two-by-six × 29¼″ (side braces)
- two-by-six × 17″
- 2″ drive screws
- 1″ or 1¼″ drive screws
- construction adhesive
- ⅜″ staples, at least fifty
- two 10d nails (cut off points)
- two-by-four × 16″
- 16½″ × 2″ × 72″ foam padding
- paint or enamel
- 28″ × 84″ heavy-duty vinyl
- 24″ × 4″ nylon or canvas webbing
- eight 1¼″ No. 10 or No. 12 round-head wood screws

Tools

- circular saw or handsaw
- scroll, jig, or coping saw
- drill, 1¼″, 5/32″ bits
- 100-grit sandpaper

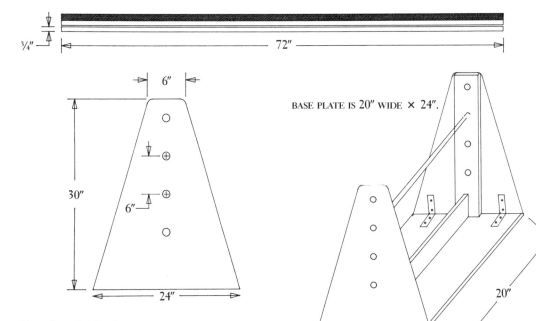

52-1. *Slant board side view.*

BASE PLATE IS 20″ WIDE × 24″.

52-2. *Slant board support.*

Cut the materials to size. Start by assembling the flat sit-up board. This means placing the foam over the top of one board, covering it with heavy-duty vinyl, with at least a 3″ overlap. The vinyl is stapled every 3″ along one side with the proper overlap, and then is pulled tight along the other side and stapled there every 3″. After that, the ends are folded over, pulled tight, and stapled every 3″ or less.

The second piece of plywood is now aligned and screwed in place with 1¼″ wood screws run in at 6″ intervals along the outside edges, and in a single seam up the center. Do *not* use wood glue here, because you may wish, eventually, to remove the bottom to replace the cover.

Screw the 16″ two-by-four side flat across the bottom side of one end of the sit-up board, using 2″ screws, and use the No. 10 or No. 12 screws to screw the webbing in place just above that.

Cut the sides from a 24″ base width to a 6″ top width, and radius the top corners (1″ radius). Install the two-by-six supports upright on the sides, ¾″ up from the bottom, using 1¼″ screws and construction adhesive. Draw a midline mark starting down 3″, and draw center marks for four holes, spaced 6″ apart, on center. Drill 1¼″ holes.

Assemble the sides to the bottom using the 3″ corner angles, and then install the center brace.

Drill the ends of the 1¼″ dowel to accept the pointless 10d nails. Insert the dowel through two holes, and support the end of the sit-up board on the dowel, with the two-by-four hooked over the dowel.

53 ✦ **Fireplace Bench**

This project goes together quickly, and serves a number of purposes: the open undersides may be used to hold kindling and small amounts of firewood, plus newspapers. The top, of course, serves as a place to sit in front of the fire.

Materials
- ¾″ × 4′ × 8′ hardwood plywood
- 12′ oak stair nosing
- 8d finishing nails
- 9′ plywood edging tape
- wood glue
- filler pencil
- polyurethane
- 21½″ × 45″ × 3″ covered cushion

Tools
- circular saw
- saw guide
- measuring tape
- square
- hammer
- nail set
- brush
- pad sander, 120-grit sandpaper
- tack cloth
- masking tape

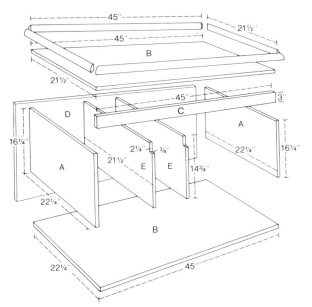

53-1. *Fireplace bench. (Courtesy of Georgia-Pacific Corporation.)*

Draw the pieces on the plywood, keeping the best side of the plywood down (even hardwood plywood has a best side). You may want to back cut lines with masking tape to reduce splintering. Cut the pieces. Mark part B as to where sections marked E will attach. Notch the E sections to take part C (¾" × 3" high notch). Start by attaching the A and C sections to one B, nailing and gluing carefully. Attach the next B section. Next attach C section to the A sections, and then slip in and attach the E sections. Attach section D next, adding in both B sections. Mitre the corners of the stair nosing to create the trim pieces on the top B section, and cover exposed plywood edges with veneer tape.

Sand well, but carefully, and finish with at least three coats of polyurethane. When finish is dry, place the cushion, and use.

54 ♦ Quick Shelves

This shelf set, almost Shaker in its simplicity, is quickly built and easily installed.

Materials
- two one-by-twelve × 8′ No. 1 pine
- twenty-four No. 8 × 1½" flathead wood screws
- eight No. 10 × 2½" flathead wood screws
- eight ⅜" × 3" toggle bolts (for hollow walls)
- 32 round-top plugs (to cover screws)
- stain
- tung oil

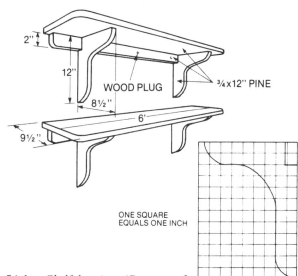

54-1. *Shelf drawing. (Courtesy of Georgia-Pacific Corporation.)*

Tools
- circular or table saw
- handsaw
- scroll saw or jigsaw
- tape measure
- square
- level
- power drill
- finishing sander, 120-grit sandpaper
- 1" graph paper

Start by ripping the one-by-twelve to 9½" wide. The 2" strips ripped off become the back braces (alternatively, you may buy one-by-ten lumber and add one-by-three for back braces: that is ⅝" wider, which makes only a minor pattern change where the braces are notched).

54-2. *Quick shelves. (Courtesy of Georgia-Pacific Corporation.)*

67

Cut to 6′ lengths and cut the wide cut-offs into 12″ lengths. These are the braces, after the pattern is traced on, and the notch is made. Notch size is 2″ × ¾″.

Cut shelving to 3′ lengths, and cut a corner of 1″ radius for the back brace and front shelf corners using a jigsaw or scroll saw. Assemble the back brace flush with the shelves using the No. 8 screws, after drilling pilot holes and countersinking. Attach the shelf brackets in the same manner.

Sand and finish the shelves. You may fill screw holes with plugs before finishing.

Install shelves with toggle bolts (in hollow walls, where no studs are present), or with long screws. Use the level to get the shelves up properly.

---

55 ♦ Serving Tray

This is a fast-to-make tray with a plywood bottom. It requires little in the way of materials, and is very useful after finishing.

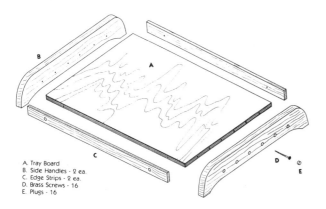

A. Tray Board
B. Side Handles - 2 ea.
C. Edge Strips - 2 ea.
D. Brass Screws - 16
E. Plugs - 16

55-1. Serving tray exploded drawing. (Courtesy of Dremel.)

Select the wood, of good grade cabinet plywood, preferably lumber core (it holds screws best). Matching or contrasting woods may be selected for other pieces.

Cut the handles following the pattern. Clamp the two pieces of wood together (or tape them together), and cut both at once. Finish shaping the handles with sandpaper, still doing both at once. Cut the edge pieces, and sand all pieces well, going at least to 180 grit sandpaper. Make sure the edges of handles are rounded, using sandpaper, and give the edge pieces a very slight rounding on their top sides.

Clamp the handles to the tray board and drill holes, as shown. Release the clamp and add glue, then screw the handles in place. Do the same with the edge pieces.

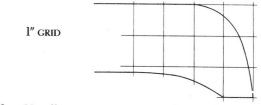

1″ GRID

55-2. Handle pattern. (Courtesy of Dremel.)

Materials
- ½″ × 13¾″ × 20″ hardwood plywood (tray board)
- two ¾″ × 3″ × 16½″ (side handles)
- two ⅜″ × 1¼″ × 20″ (edge strips)
- sixteen No. 8 × 2″ flathead wood screws
- sixteen ⅜″ wood plugs
- wood glue
- stain
- clear finish

Tools
- circular, hand, or table saw
- scroll saw or jigsaw
- screwdriver
- drill
- finishing sander, 150 and 180 grit sandpaper
- measuring tape
- square
- two 24″ bar clamps

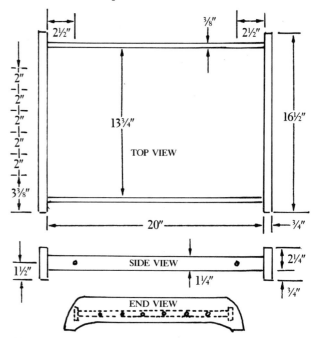

55-3. Plan drawing. (Courtesy of Dremel.)

Let the glue dry, scrape off any squeeze-out, and lightly finish-sand the tray. Clean with a tack cloth, and stain. Coat with a clear finish of your choice.

5 · Additional General Plans

This chapter is presented separately to give you a break from the first four chapters. The projects are similar in scope to those in Chapter 4.

56 ✦ Napkin Holder

A friend, Paul Meisel, provided some samples of salt and pepper shakers that gave the opportunity to solve one of my favorite gripes: the napkin holder, with salt and pepper set, that shortchanges one end of the informal table. I used solid cherry, and saved work with spindles and carved hearts available commercially.

56-1.   *Napkin holder.*

Materials
- one-by-six × 9½″ cherry (or other wood)
- 1″ × 1¾″ × 6″ cherry
- eight 3″ (plus tenons) spindles
- two 1″ carved hearts
- four shakers
- spray satin polyurethane
- wood glue

Start by cutting the bottom blank to size, and then add the napkin holder tops. These are now marked for the holes to be drilled, with the ¼″ brad point bit used to drill ⅜″ deep for tenons set ½″ in from each edge, in a line 3″ from each end. The next tenon is 1″ over from there. Set the next two holes in line with holes from the opposite edge.

56-2.   *Use Forstner bit to drill shaker holes.*

Tools
- saw
- drill, ¼″ brad point, 1¼″ Forstner bits
- router, ⅜″ round-over bit
- mallet
- sander, 100- and 150-grit sandpaper

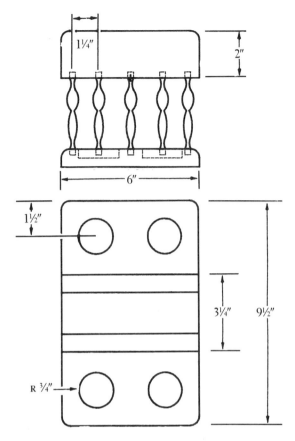

The 1¼″ holes that hold the shakers are ⅜″ deep also, and are drilled 1¾″ in from each side and each end. Hearts are epoxied in place between holes, with the heart upper edges touching the routed round-over line. Do rounding over before doing any gluing of hearts or spindles! Sand lightly before assembly, with both grits.

Once the round-over is done, spread glue carefully on tenons and in holes, starting with the base, one assembly at a time. Set spindles in the base, spread glue on top tenons and in top holes, align and tap into place.

After glue dries, check for excess and scrape off with a chisel or scraper. Check the fit of the shakers, remove and spray-coat the project at least twice, preferably three times.

56-3. *Napkin holder plan drawing.*

57 ◆ Turned Maple-and-Walnut Lamp

This lamp design is my friend Bobby Weaver's idea, and most of the work is his. He needed a lamp, and so we checked his shop and mine and came up with maple and walnut for contrasting woods, glued up in a pattern that would increase the contrast.

57-1. *Turned lamp.*

56-4. *Napkin holder with spindles laid out.*

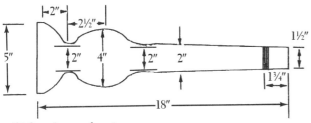

57-2. *Lamp drawing.*

Materials
- 3″ × 3″ × 18″ block of maple (can be glued up)
- four 3¾″ × ¾″ × 9″ walnut (we used 18″ lengths by mistake)
- four 4½″ × ¾″ × 9″ maple
- 6″ × 6″ × ¾″ walnut (base)
- wood glue
- bar clamps
- lamp assembly, including harp, bulb holder, 18″ pipe, cord

Tools
- lathe, large gouge, skew
- parting tool
- calipers
- measuring tape
- square
- heavy mallet
- power sander
- 120-grit sandpaper strips
- steel wool
- tung oil
- tack cloth
- glue brush or other spreader

Start by making sure all parts fit well. We glued up the 3″ × 3″ block needed using 1½″ × 3½″ maple, which had to be squared back. Glue was scraped and the walnut mounted. After that, the glue was scraped, the final maple was mounted.

All glue was allowed to dry at least overnight, under full clamp pressure, to develop the best bond possible for safe turning.

Bobby chucked the blank, after the ends were squared and centers found, and began turning with a gouge. He turned to the pattern that shows in the photograph. If you turn to a slightly different shape, you'll get a varied pattern.

57-3. *Overnight clamping is best when glued-up object is to be turned.*

57-4. *Use care to line up tool holder, start at wide end.*

57-5. *Once wide end maple is rounded, move on to narrow end.*

57-6. *Patterns begin to show.*

If you change the order of woods, or the types of woods, the pattern will vary once again. This type of turning provides an almost unlimited number of variants simply by changing the center wood color, or the wood color on all, or any, of the glue-ups.

We used a drill press and an 18″ bell ringer's bit to drill the hole for the pipe. This is time-consuming, regardless of bit sharpness or drill power. If the bit is buried too deep in each bite, it heats up and may crack the narrower portions of the neck—it may also ruin an expensive drill bit. Drill bits do not have the long swirls up the full length needed to carry cuttings up and out, so the bit must be backed out after every ½″ to ¾″ of drilling.

The base blank is cut to 6″ square, and a 1½″ hole is drilled to mate with the pipe hole at the base of the turning (this will drift off some if you force the bit, so check to be sure). Starting at the area to be the back of the lamp, rout a ½″ deep by ½″ wide slot into the center hole. This allows the cord to run out without tipping the lamp.

57-7 *Base is ready for mounting.*

Square the turning base and top on the sander, and mount the square base with wood glue. Wipe on at least three coats of tung oil, after a thorough sanding and cleaning. Break the surface on the first two coats with steel wool.

Install the hardware, and find a shade. You've got a one-of-a-kind lamp (even if you followed our pattern almost exactly, yours will differ some).

58 ◆ Tool Stand

This is a fairly easy-to-build tool stand. At its particular height, it's perfect for a small table saw. Height is easily varied by lengthening, or shortening, the legs.

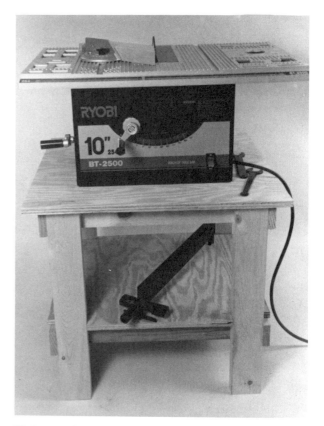

58-1. *Tool stand.*

Materials
- ¾″ × 24″ × 24″ plywood (top)
- ¾″ × 24″ × 20″ plywood (shelf)
- four two-by-four × 24″ (legs)
- four two-by-four × 21″ (leg braces)
- four two-by-four × 20″ (inside leg braces)
- 2″ drive screws
- 1¼″ drive screws

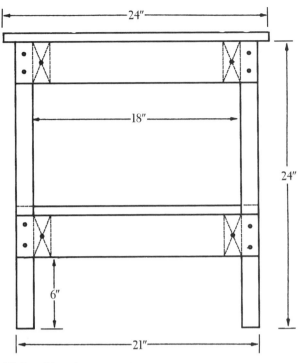

58-2. *Plan drawing.*

Tools
- wood rasp
- circular saw or table saw
- drill, ⅛" bit
- Phillips driver bit

Start by cutting all pieces to size, and assembling the leg unit with longer braces placed outside the legs, on the sides, to form double-leg units first. The shorter braces then go on the inside, forming the base unit. The shelf is notched to fit and installed using 1¼" drive screws.

Position the top and fasten down with at least eight 1¼" drive screws. Use a wood rasp to remove any burrs. I didn't finish this one, but you may if you wish.

59 ◆ Cedar Music Box

My wife expressed an interest in a cedar box we saw in my uncle's antique store outside Charlottesville, so I decided to do a version of the box. This is *not* a reproduction of anything—and I doubt the box we saw was old enough or good enough to warrant such attention.

59-1. *Cedar box.*

Start by gluing up the pieces to form the top and bottom. I glued this up a bit oversize to allow for using the jointer and table saw to even things up. Once the glue dries, joint the edges and square up the corners to get the final sizes.

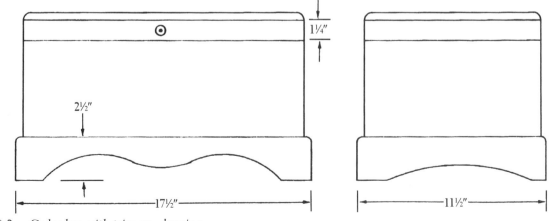

59-2. *Cedar box with trim on, drawing.*

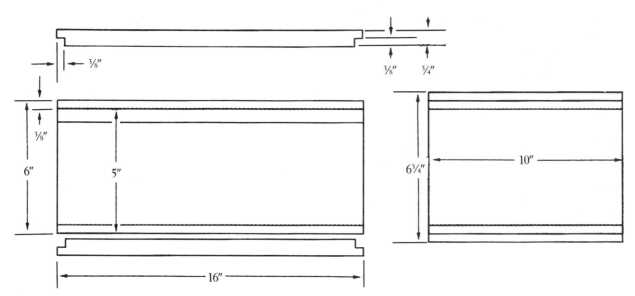

59-3. *Cedar box without trim, drawing.*

Materials

- two 7½″ × 1″ × 16″ cedar (front and back)
- two 7½″ × 1″ × 10″ cedar (sides)
- two 17½″ × 1″ × 3″ cedar (front and back trim)
- two 11½″ × 1″ × 3″ cedar (side trim)
- two 10″ × 16″ × 1″ cedar (top and bottom)
- twelve joiner biscuits
- wood glue
- two H hinges, black
- 1″ porcelain knob, white
- tung oil

Tools

- table saw
- mitre saw
- biscuit joiner
- router, ⅜″ round-over, ⅜″ rabbetting bits
- scroll, jig, or band saw
- band clamp
- two 24″ bar clamps
- measuring tape
- square
- screwdriver
- mallet
- drill, ³⁄₃₂″ bit
- sander, 100- and 180-grit sandpaper

59-4. *Routed ⅜″ × ⅜″ rabbet.*

With the router, rout one side of all top and bottom edges with a ⅜″ × ⅜″ rabbet. Now, do the same with the materials for the front, back, and sides, routing both the tops and bottoms, and making sure the top and bottom rabbets are on the same side.

Mitre the sides and front and back. Set up the biscuit joiner to work with mitres and slot for biscuits about 1½″ in from each end—make sure to get the joiner properly settled before making the cut. Check dry-fit with biscuits.

74

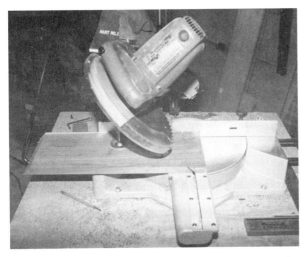

59-5. *Long-edge mitres are very easily done with slide-action compound mitre saw such as this Makita.*

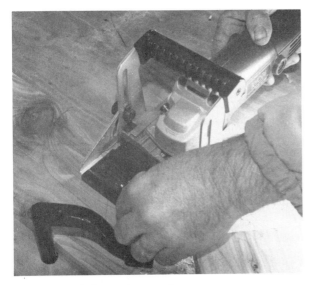

59-6. *Carefully cut biscuit slots.*

59-7. *Box assembly.*

Assemble two corners at the same end with biscuits and glue, and then assemble the final two corners. Check square and use the band clamp on the middle of the structure to pull things up tight. Check square again. Let the glue dry.

Check fit of the top and bottom and make any needed adjustments. Glue the top and bottom in place to make an enclosed box.

When the glue has dried, rout the round-over on the top, and place masking tape around the area to be cut. Assemble some ⅛″ shims, and set the rip fence to allow you to cut off the top. Top depth left on box is 1⅜″. Cut one long side, then the other, with the saw set to cut about ⅞″ deep (actual thickness of the wood is ¾″). Cut one end loose, and shim. Cut the other end loose, working with even more care to keep the cut from twisting.

You now have a box and top. Round over the tops of the decorative pieces, and go on to cut the pattern in the trim using a scroll, jig, or band saw. Mitre their ends and slot for a single biscuit, centered.

59-8. *Roundover is cut after glue-up of box.*

59-9. *Mask cut line, and rip on saw, using ⅛″ shims to keep cut line spread (it may be necessary to tape shims in place, too).*

Assemble around the base of the box, setting the box up on scrap stock until the bottom is even with the highest point of the pattern in the trim. Use the band clamp again.

Sand carefully, after scraping off excess glue. Cedar sands down in a rush, so don't press too hard. Use a tack cloth to remove dust, and then coat with tung oil. Break the surface between coats with steel wool, and apply at least two coats.

59-10. *The band clamp holds trim in place very well.*

59-11. *Finish with tung oil.*

Install hardware, and the job is almost done. To make this a music box, I drilled a ½″ × 1½″ hole in the underside of one bottom corner. A ¼″ hole came up into the box from underneath that, and there was then plenty of room for the music movement key.

60 ◆ Miniature Piano Music Box

A music box styled as an upright piano makes a lovely gift for any occasion or none. This version is of walnut, with bubinga hardwood trim, a keyboard, and music movement, available commercially

60-1. *Piano music box.*

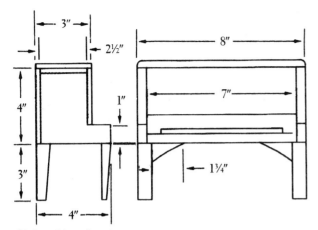

60-2. *Plan drawing.*

60-3. *Box being assembled.*

Materials

- ½″ × 3″ × 8″ bubinga (underside, keyboard carriage)
- 7″ × ½″ × 4″ walnut (front)
- 8″ × ½″ × 4″ walnut (back)
- 8″ × ½″ × 3″ walnut (top)
- two 4″ × ½″ × 2½″ walnut (sides)
- two 1″ × ¾″ × 3″ walnut (front legs)
- two 1″ × ¾″ × 5″ walnut (back legs)
- two ¾″ × 1¾″ × 1½″ walnut (front leg braces)
- ¼″ × 7″ × 1″ bubinga (music holder)
- keyboard and music movement
- wood glue
- epoxy

Tools

- saw
- router, ¼″ rabbetting, ¼″ round-over bits
- drill, ¼″ drill bit
- tenon saw
- ½″ chisel
- pad sander, 100- and 150-grit sandpaper
- light bar clamps
- C-clamps

60-4. *Note taper on legs as one leg is made ready for cut that will form joint with back.*

Start by cutting all materials to size, planing wood down where needed.

Rout the top edges of sides, front, and back to a ¼″ depth and a ¼″ width. Rout the top edges the same size, as well as the back edges of the sides, and the upper front edges. Sides are first cut to an L shape, as the drawing shows. Do not rout the lower edge of the L.

Assemble the basic box and check fit. Reassemble and glue, with clamps. Make sure box is square.

Cut tapers in legs, bringing the taper from the full width of 1″ at 3″ height down to ½″ width at the bottom. Taper on one side only, to face the front on all legs. Do *not* taper the upper 2″ on the rear legs.

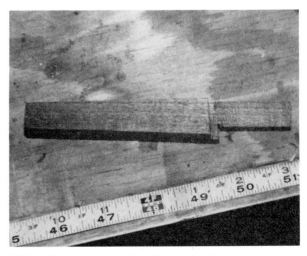

60-5. *Legs are notched to fit into back.*

60-6. *Legs, glued and clamped.*

Cut across the rear legs to a ⅜″ depth, leaving 3″ standing height, and chisel off ⅜″ of material remaining on the upper part. This gives a flat surface to fit against the insides of the back, where the leg is clamped and glued. Legs are glued on at the same time, using either no clamps and epoxy glue, or very light bar clamps and wood glue. Glue in the front leg braces before handling the remaining unit much.

60-7. *Music movement ready to go in box.*

Drill ¼″ hole for key shaft for music box movement. This is best placed so that there is 2″ clearance on all sides. Dry-fit the top and rout the round-over with it dry-fitted, or rout the round-over with the top on a routing pad.

Install the music movement, without its key. Glue the box lid in place. Finish the box, using 100 and 150 grit sandpaper, and your choice of clear finishes. I recommend not staining woods such as walnut. Lay a piece of ¾″ masking tape over the keyboard area before finishing. Let finish dry, peel off masking tape, and epoxy the keyboard in place. Insert the music movement key and the box is done.

61 ♦ Divider Shelves

These quick-to-build shelves are designed to also serve as a divider unit: the width is variable, but 32″ is the maximum for each shelf unit. As presented, all shelves are permanently mounted for stability; you may, as the photo shows, leave out a center shelf, if you wish. Basic materials are for one unit, unless otherwise indicated.

61-1. *Divider shelves. (Courtesy of Georgia-Pacific Corporation.)*

Materials
- four one-by-four × 8′
- four one-by-three × 8′
- two one-by-ten × 8′
- No. 8 × 1¾″ flathead wood drive screws
- 6d finishing nails
- 4″ hinges (one pair per pair of divider units)
- wood glue
- 120-grit sandpaper

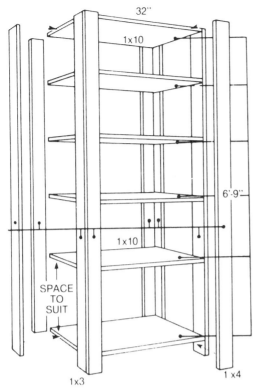

61-2. *Divider shelf drawing. (Courtesy of Georgia-Pacific Corporation.)*

Tools
- handsaw or circular saw
- drill, clutched, with screwdriver bit
- hammer
- nail set
- square
- finishing sander
- clear finish, 3″ brush

Begin by cutting uprights to length. If you have fairly high ceilings, just square the ends of the 8′ material. For the rest of us, the uprights should probably be limited to 84″ high. Nail (with 6d finishing nails) and glue the uprights together, with one-by-three and one-by-four stock forming an L with equal sides. Make four uprights for each unit desired.

Decide on shelf width and the number of shelves, and then decide on placement. Usually, at least 12″ between shelves is considered reasonable. I suggest starting with a 17″ or 18″ space for the bottom shelf, and dividing the remainder nearly equally.

Drill pilot holes for two screws each in the front and side of each part of each upright, and run in the No. 8 drive screws. Make sure the assembly is square as you go, for this thing isn't going to change too easily once it's made.

If several units are to be made and used as a divider, hinge them together with butt hinges, with removable pins, surface-mounted on one side. Use two hinges per pair of uprights. Finish before installing the hinges.

62 ♦ Redwood Shelves

We were in our usual situation—too many books, not enough shelves—when I discovered some one-by-ten redwood I had left in my shop. Redwood usually isn't considered strong in the ways needed in book shelving, but there are methods to allow for that; so I built a pair of these shelves.

62-1. *Redwood bookshelves.*

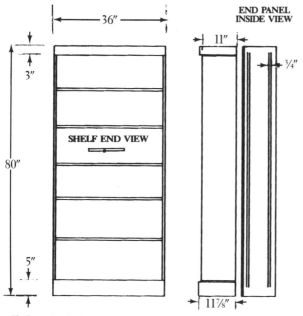

SHELF END VIEW

62-2. *Shelf drawing.*

Materials
- two one-by-ten × 8′ redwood, clear heart
- two one-by-ten × 12′ redwood, clear heart
- five 1″ × 1½″ × 35″ fir
- one-by-four × 6′ redwood, clear heart
- one-by-six × 6′ redwood, clear heart
- ¼″ × 4′ × 8′ hardboard
- 2d finishing nails
- 6d finishing nails
- wood glue
- 5′ shelf standards
- shelf clips
- polyurethane

Tools
- mitre box
- table saw, with dado set (optional)
- router, cove bit
- hammer
- measuring tape
- framing square
- try square
- combination square
- nail set

Start by cutting side boards and top boards to size. The unit is 82″ tall, with the top board set 2½″ inside that, in ¾″ dadoes. The bottom shelf is set 5½″ up from the bottom (top edge) in another ¾″ dado. These dadoes may be run with a table saw or with a router: both are ⅜″ deep. Top pieces are 35¼″ wide to give a 36″ side-to-side width (plus 1½″ for trim pieces top and bottom).

Cut five shelf pieces 34″ wide. Make two dadoes on the *inside* of each side board, with the front dado 1½″ in from the edge and the back dado 2″ in from the back edge. These must be mirror images, as must the dadoes for top and bottom pieces.

Down the center of each shelf make a ⅜″ deep dado. Into these, glue and clamp the ¾″ wide fir strips. The fir strips add the small bit of "backbone" needed to support a full load of heavy books.

Cut a ¼″ deep × ⅜″ wide rabbet around all back edges (remember, the top and bottom horizontal pieces are going to be in closer than the actual edges, and must be rabbeted as well). Cut the ¼″ × 4′ × 8′ board to fit in this space. Assemble top, bottom, and both sides with 6d finishing nails and glue; the nails are only to keep things from drifting as you work on one end or another of a fairly large assembly. Use one or two nails per board end until you can get back with clamps.

Clamp securely and check for square. You may use the framing square, or measure diagonals to check the square.

When glue is dry, place the backboard, with glue on top and bottom edges, but *not* on sides. Use 2d finishing nails at 6″ intervals to fasten in place.

Sand and finish. I used flat polyurethane on mine, and am delighted with the soft glow the redwood took on. It is an unusual bookcase material, too, so it draws comment.

Install the shelf standards and clips. Install shelves. Load. They'll take almost anything with that fir spine in place.

63 ♦ Decorated Splined Frames

My friend Bobby Weaver sometimes gets experimental. He wanted to see how joiner biscuits would look partially exposed in these frames. He was also curious about appearance in using walnut and cherry in different combinations, so he worked up two frames that mirror each other's colors.

Materials
- four 2″ × 1″ × 16″ walnut
- four 2″ × 1″ × 16″ cherry
- four 16″ × ⅜″ rounded cherry
- four 16″ × ⅜″ rounded walnut
- four 16″ × ¼″ rounded cherry
- four 16″ × ¼″ rounded walnut
- eight joiner biscuits
- wood glue

- tung oil
- 120-grit sandpaper
- saw-tooth hanger

Tools
- table saw
- mitre box
- router, ⅜″ and ¼″ core bits, ⅜″ rabbetting bit
- router edge guide
- square
- measuring tape

63-1. *Splined frames.*

Make routed coves on all pieces, after cutting ⅜″ × ⅜″ rabbets on the backs of the pieces, and then cut to size. Round the small stock to fit coves starting with a round-over bit on a router. Do this with larger stock, which is then ripped loose with the table saw and finished by hand.

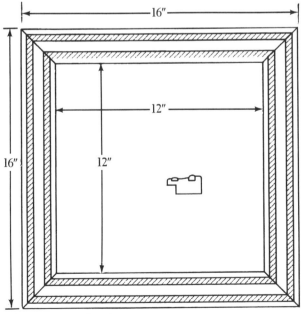

63-2. *Frame drawing.*

63-3. *Note light color of beech joiner biscuit against darker wood color.*

Mount the contrasting color strips in the core holes with wood glue. Clamp for at least two hours.

Mitre corners to suit. Set table saw depth to half the thickness of the stock, and space it one-third the distance of the material from the rip fence. Rip spline slots.

Install joiner biscuits in the spline slots when gluing up the mitres. Cut and sand the biscuits after the glue has dried. Sand the entire unit, after scraping off excess glue. Coat with tung oil, and install hanger, glass, mat, and so on.

64 and 65 ◆ Towel Holder and Recipe– Cookbook Holder

Kitchens are usually only neat in magazine articles. There are cookbooks and recipe cards and spilled thises and thats all over most of those I've seen. These two projects provide room for cookbooks, recipe cards, and a spot to put the paper towels to wipe up the spills.

64 and 65-1. *Two kitchen helper projects. (Courtesy of Georgia-Pacific Corporation.)*

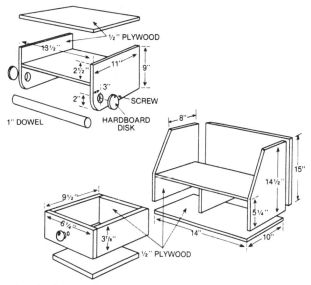

64 and 65-2.   Plan drawings. (Courtesy of Georgia-Pacific Corporation.)

Materials

- 4′ × 4′ × ½″ A-B or A-C interior plywood
- 1″ × 13″ hardwood dowel
- 2d finishing nails
- wood filler
- enamel
- two porcelain or brass knobs
- four 1½″ × No. 6 round-head wood screws
- two 2″ diameter hardboard scraps
- No. 6 × ⅝″ round-head wood screws
- 120-grit sandpaper
- wood glue

Tools

- circular saw
- scroll saw or jigsaw
- square
- measuring tape
- drill, 1¹⁄₁₆″ Forstner drill bit
- finishing sander
- paint brush
- hammer
- nail set

Make the towel holder with a 12½″ interior width to allow standard paper towel rolls to turn freely. The exterior, then, is 13½″ with ½″ plywood. Cut the top 13½″ × 12″. The 1″ lip gives a place for you to screw the unit into the underside of your cabinets; you may also use brass angle supports and screw it in from the sides. Cut the shelf 12½″ × 11″, and set the shelf 2½″ down from the top. Cut two sides, each 9″ × 12″, and round the lower forward corner on a 1½″ radius.

Drill the 1¹⁄₁₆″ holes to accept the 1″ dowel for the towels 2″ up from the bottom of the side and 3″ back from the front. Assemble the top, sides, and shelf using 2d nails and wood glue. Make sure the unit is square. Attach one disc of hardboard (2″ diameter, cut with the scroll saw) permanently to one side, and suspend the other from a No. 6 × ⅝″ round-head wood screw. Sand, clean, and paint.

The recipe–cookbook holder starts with a back 14″ wide by 15″ high. The bottom is 14″ wide by 10″ deep, and sides are 10″ deep by 14½″ wide, tapering to 8″ at the top, from the 5¼″ mark on the front side. The shelf is 10″ deep and 13″ wide. Sand and assemble all pieces with 2d nails and glue, checking square as you go.

Cut drawer parts in tandem: fronts are 6¼″ × 3⅞″; four sides are 9″ × 3⅞″; backs are 5¼″ × 3⅞″. Cut both bottoms 5½″ × 8½″. Use ¾″ brads to nail the drawers together, with glue. Sand. Drill knob holes, paint, and install the knobs.

66 and 67 ♦ Cabinet and Curio Cabinet

These two projects provide useful cabinetry for many needs, and may be wall-mounted or placed on top of a table, desk or similar stand. Both are straightforward, but they each take a little time. Both are more easily made with a table saw, but a router and circular saw may be used, with great care.

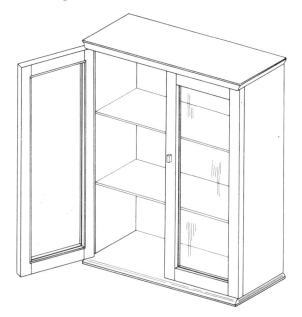

66 and 67-1.   Cabinet. (Courtesy of Dremel.)

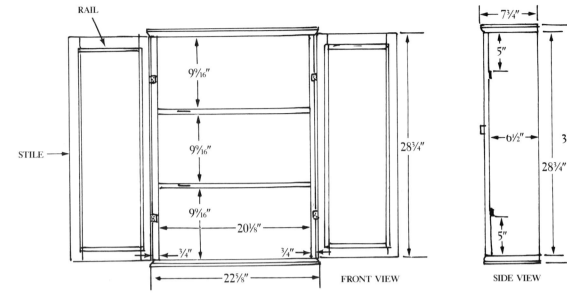

66 and 67-2. *Plan drawing. (Courtesy of Dremel.)*

Materials

Large cabinet:

- $\frac{7}{8}'' \times 7\frac{3}{4}'' \times 22\frac{5}{8}''$ (top)
- $\frac{7}{8}'' \times 7\frac{3}{4}'' \times 22\frac{5}{8}''$ (bottom)
- two $\frac{3}{4}'' \times 6\frac{1}{2}'' \times 28\frac{3}{4}''$ (sides)
- $\frac{3}{8}'' \times 20\frac{3}{4}'' \times 29\frac{5}{16}''$ (back panel)
- four $\frac{3}{4}'' \times 1\frac{3}{4}'' \times 7\frac{7}{8}''$ (door rails)
- four $\frac{3}{4}'' \times 1\frac{1}{2}'' \times 28\frac{3}{4}''$ (door stiles)
- four $\frac{1}{4}'' \times \frac{1}{4}'' \times 8\frac{3}{4}''$ (rail moulding strips)
- four $\frac{1}{4}'' \times \frac{1}{4}'' \times 26\frac{1}{8}''$ (stile moulding strips)
- thirty-six $\frac{3}{8}'' \times 2''$ dowels
- ten No. 6 $\times$ 1" flathead wood screws
- two wall hangers, $\frac{1}{8}'' \times \frac{3}{4}'' \times 2''$
- two $\frac{3}{16}'' \times 6'' \times 20''$ shelves, wood or glass
- eight $\frac{1}{8}'' \times 1''$ shelf-support dowels
- two door handles
- four brass door hinges, $1\frac{1}{2}'' \times 1''$
- $\frac{3}{4}''$ brass nails

Tools

- table saw, dado blade set
- circular saw
- saw guide
- router, $\frac{3}{8}''$ and $\frac{1}{4}''$ rabbetting bit
- edge guide
- glass cutter
- dowel centers ($\frac{3}{8}''$, $\frac{1}{8}''$ for large cabinet, $\frac{1}{4}''$, $\frac{1}{8}''$ for curio)
- measuring tape
- square
- hammer
- drill, $\frac{3}{8}''$ and $\frac{1}{4}''$ brad point drill bit, $\frac{1}{8}''$ drill bit

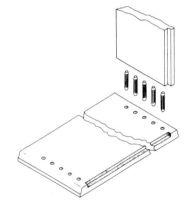

66 and 67-3. *Dowel setup. (Courtesy of Dremel.)*

Curio cabinet:

- $\frac{3}{4}'' \times 4\frac{5}{8}'' \times 15\frac{1}{8}''$ (top)
- $\frac{3}{4}'' \times 4\frac{5}{8}'' \times 15\frac{1}{8}''$ (bottom)
- two $\frac{1}{2}'' \times 4\frac{15}{16}'' \times 19\frac{3}{16}''$ (sides)
- $\frac{1}{4}'' \times 13\frac{27}{32}'' \times 19\frac{9}{16}''$ (back)
- four $\frac{1}{2}'' \times 1\frac{1}{4}'' \times 4\frac{7}{8}''$ (door rails)
- four $\frac{1}{2}'' \times 1'' \times 19\frac{3}{16}''$ (door stiles)
- four $\frac{3}{16}'' \times \frac{3}{16}'' \times 5\frac{27}{32}''$ (rail moulding strips)
- four $\frac{3}{16}'' \times \frac{3}{16}'' \times 17\frac{7}{16}''$ (stile moulding strips)
- thirty-six $\frac{1}{4}'' \times 1\frac{1}{4}''$ dowels
- ten No. 6 $\times$ $\frac{3}{4}''$ flathead wood screws
- two wall hangers, $\frac{1}{8}'' \times \frac{1}{2}'' \times 1\frac{3}{8}''$
- two $\frac{1}{4}'' \times 4'' \times 13\frac{5}{16}''$ shelves, wood or glass
- eight $\frac{1}{8}'' \times 1''$ shelf-support dowels
- two door handles
- two brass door hinges, $1'' \times \frac{3}{4}''$
- $\frac{1}{2}''$ brad nails

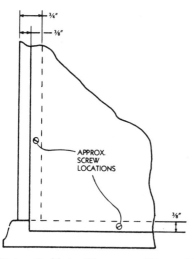

66 and 67-4.   *Rabbets. (Courtesy of Dremel.)*

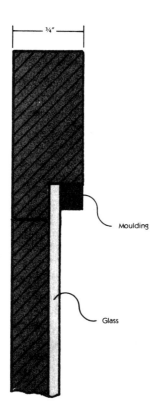

66 and 67-5.   *Cross section of door frame. (Courtesy of Dremel.)*

66 and 67-6.   *Moulding types. (Courtesy of Dremel.)*

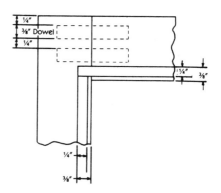

66 and 67-7.   *Typical door frame. (Courtesy of Dremel.)*

Cut all pieces to correct dimensions, and sand smooth. Measure and mark all dowel holes and drill. Mark the corresponding dowel positions using dowel centers, mark, and drill. Cut rabbet in the sides. Cut stopped rabbet in the bottom and top. Cut the back piece. Glue dowels into side pieces and allow to dry.

Check moulding needs for the top and bottom pieces. If any are desired, cut to size.

Put the back, sides, top, and bottom together without glue. Use small brads to temporarily fasten. Cut rabbets in the rails, and cut stopped rabbets in the stiles.

Drill dowel holes in the rails and stiles and glue all pieces together, clamping well, and making sure of square. Attach door handles. Test-assemble the doors in the cabinet.

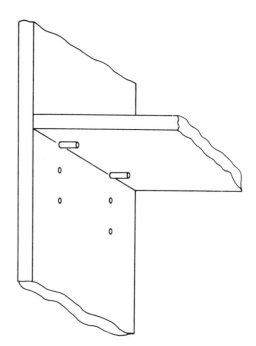

66 and 67-8.   *Shelf support. (Courtesy of Dremel.)*

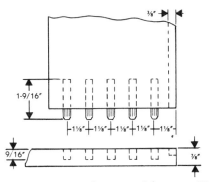

66 and 67-9. *Dowel for top and bottom. (Courtesy of Dremel.)*

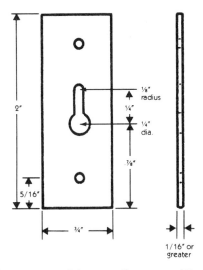

66 and 67-10. *Wall hanger. (Courtesy of Dremel.)*

Take the cabinet apart, measure, and mark shelf positions. Make adjustments about 1½" apart. Drill holes to allow adjustable shelving.

Glue up cabinet parts, now, clamping well and allowing sufficient drying time for the glue. Mortise hinges into cabinet and doors.

Make and attach wall hangers to cabinet back. Finish-sand, and finish with stain and tung oil or other clear finish.

Install glass in the doors using moulding strips, and then install shelves of wood or glass.

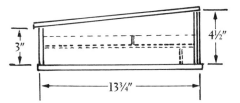

68-1. *Lap desk plan drawing. (Courtesy of Dremel.)*

68 ♦ Walnut Lap Desk

Lap desks are excellent gift items, and are also useful to have around one's own home. This version, made in walnut, may be made in other woods, but has a particular rich appearance in that wood.

Tools
- hand, table, or radial-arm saw
- mitre box
- plane
- four corner clamps
- lightweight 24" or 18" bar clamps
- router or rotary tool, ⅛" straight bit
- small screwdriver
- hand or push drill, drill point
- ⅛" cabinetmaker's chisel
- sander

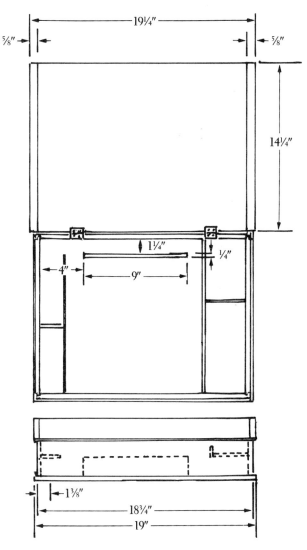

Materials

- 3″ × 18¾″ × ⅜″ (front)
- 4½″ × 18¾″ × ⅜″ (back)
- 3″ × 13¼″ × ⅜″ (side)
- 4½″ × 13¼″ × ⅜″ (side)
- 14¼″ × 19″ × ⅜″ (top)
- two ⅝″ × 14¼″ × ⅜″ (breadboard edges)
- 14⅛″ × 19″ × ⅜″ (bottom)
- four ½″ × ½″ × 3/16″ (feet, felt)
- 1⅞″ × 13¼″ × ⅛″ (left side tray bottom)
- ½″ × 13″ × ⅛″ (left side tray side)
- ⅜″ × 1⅞″ × ⅛″ (divider)
- 3⅜″ × 13¼″ × ⅛″ (right side tray bottom)
- 1″ × 13″ × ⅛″ (right side tray side)
- ⅞″ × 3⅛″ × ⅛″ (divider)
- 1½″ × 9″ × ¼″ (letter holder)
- two 13/16″ × 1″ hinges
- ten No. 2 × ⅜″ screws for trays
- six ⅛″ × ¾″ dowels
- 120- and 180-grit sandpaper
- sealer
- wood glue
- clear finish

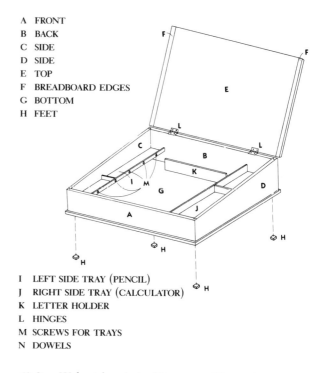

A   FRONT
B   BACK
C   SIDE
D   SIDE
E   TOP
F   BREADBOARD EDGES
G   BOTTOM
H   FEET

I   LEFT SIDE TRAY (PENCIL)
J   RIGHT SIDE TRAY (CALCULATOR)
K   LETTER HOLDER
L   HINGES
M   SCREWS FOR TRAYS
N   DOWELS

68-3.   *Walnut lap desk. (Courtesy of Dremel.)*

Carefully cut all pieces to size, as accurately as possible. At least a small table or radial-arm saw is recommended here, though a mitre box will do for crosscuts.

Before you do the dado and tongue-and-groove joints in walnut, I suggest you try these out in a piece of same-size pine, or some other scrap wood lying around awaiting discard. The joints are simple, but do require some patience.

Cut dadoes in front and back pieces. Cut rabbets in the sides. Assemble tray parts, and cut grooves for trays in front and back pieces (A—front; B—back). Test-assemble sides, front, and back, with trays, to check fit. If all fits, add glue and clamp for final assembly.

Top and bottom have to be glued up of narrower stock. Do so, and sand smooth, in readiness for later use.

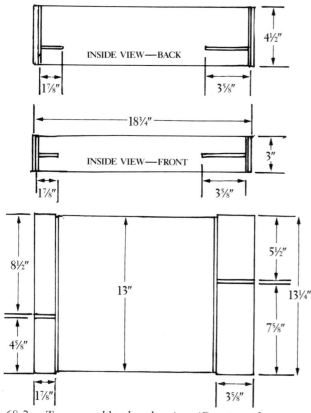

INSIDE VIEW—BACK

1⅞″   3⅝″

18¾″

INSIDE VIEW—FRONT

4½″

3″

1⅞″   3⅝″

8½″   13″   5½″

13¼″

4⅝″   7⅝″

1⅞″   3⅝″

68-2.   *Tray assembly plan drawing. (Courtesy of Dremel.)*

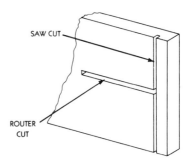

SAW CUT

ROUTER CUT

68-4.   *Dado and tray grooves. (Courtesy of Dremel.)*

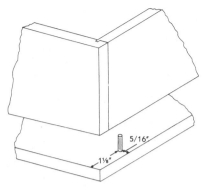

68-5. *Rabbet and dado joints. (Courtesy of Dremel.)*

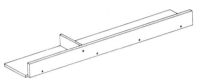

68-6. *Pencil tray. (Courtesy of Dremel.)*

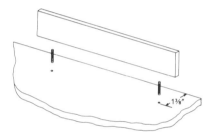

68-7. *Letter holder tray attachment to bottom. (Courtesy of Dremel.)*

Add the letter holder to the assembly and then dowel the bottom (G) to the box, using the push drill or a hand drill to come all the way through the bottom and into the sides for the dowelling. Use great care here to avoid going over the line and missing the side. Blind dowelling is possible, but unnecessary; birch dowel pins will contrast nicely with the walnut, or walnut will match.

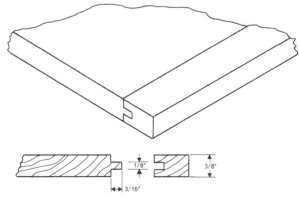

68-8. *Top assembly detail. (Courtesy of Dremel.)*

Cut breadboard tongue-and-groove for the top assembly, and glue up, clamping gently to prevent bowing. Bevel top edges of front and back to same angle as sides. Attach hinges to box, and attach to top. Finish-sand. Remove hinges and finish with tung oil, at least three coats.

69 ◆ Collector's Table

Most of us have some sort of small collection around that needs a bit of dust-resistant space for display. It's not unusual, too, to have a need for a small coffee table in the living room. This attractive project can serve both purposes.

69-1. *Collector's table. (Courtesy of Stanley Tools.)*

The illustrated table is of hardwood, which requires you either to form your own mouldings (easily done with a router and sufficient bits), or buy mouldings made to order. If you make thin mouldings, cut them on wider stock, and then rip them to final size on a table saw.

Tools
- measuring tape
- square
- four corner clamps
- drill, VSR and clutching, screwdriver bit, $1/16''$ drill bit, drill bit sized for T-nuts
- flat-blade screwdriver
- $3/4''$ wood chisel
- scribe
- handsaw, mitre box
- router, $1/2''$ straight bit

69-2. *Collector's table. (Courtesy of Stanley Tools.)*

Materials

- one-quarter sheet ¾″ hardwood or fir plywood
- two one-by-three × 6′ pine, select B or better
- two one-by-two × 6′ pine, select B or better
- two ⁹⁄₃₂″ × 1⅜″ × 6′ lattice
- two ⅜″ × ¾″ × 6′ stop
- two ¼″ × ¾″ × 6′ screen moulding
- four 12″ tapered square section legs
- four leg glides
- four T-nuts
- three 2½″ brass butt hinges, with screws
- two cabinet hooks and staples
- 35⅞″ × 19⅞″ × ¼″ plate glass (when rest of table is *finished,* measure the inside dimensions of the lid rabbet, and subtract ⅛″ in each direction to get the exact size)
- No 6 × ¾″, No. 8 × ¼″, No. 8 × 2″ flathead steel screws
- 1 lid support
- 1″ steel brads
- 37½″ × 21½″ felt
- wood glue
- wood filler
- stain
- polyurethane

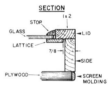

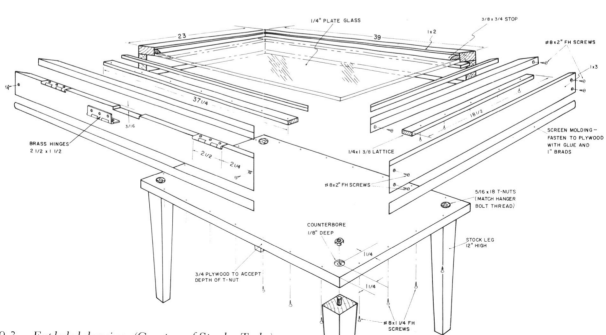

69-3. *Exploded drawing. (Courtesy of Stanley Tools.)*

Cut two pieces of one-by-three × 29″ long, with vertically mitred ends. (One-by-three stock allows a depth of about 2″ free storage. If you want more, increase stock width. You can adjust leg height by getting shorter legs, or sawing off leg ends: best table height is between 15″ and 18″.) Cut two pieces of one-by-three at 23″ long, again mitred vertically. Drill holes to countersink screw heads. Cut three hinge recesses in backboard, with each (if you use the listed hinges) 2½″ long and ³⁄₁₆″ deep. Clamp assembly together with corner clamps, checking square all the way. Do all assembly on a flat surface. Mark holes and drill. Remove clamps, place glue, and reassemble with No. 8 × 2″ screws. Reclamp and check for square.

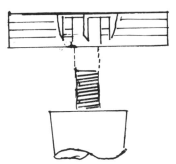

69-7.   *Install T-nut. (Courtesy of Stanley Tools.)*

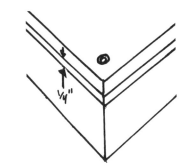

69-8.   *Install bottom. (Courtesy of Stanley Tools.)*

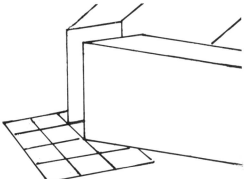

69-4.   *Vertically mitred corners. (Courtesy of Stanley Tools.)*

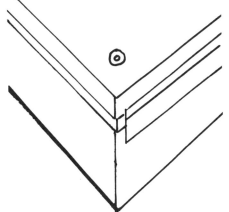

69-9.   *Add moulding. (Courtesy of Stanley Tools.)*

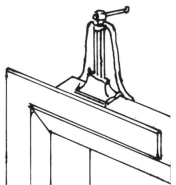

69-5.   *Square up the corner and clamp. (Courtesy of Stanley Tools.)*

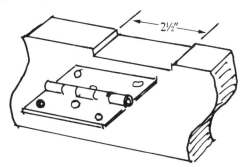

69-6.   *Cut for hinges. (Courtesy of Stanley Tools.)*

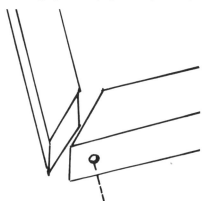

69-10.   *Make lid parts. (Courtesy of Stanley Tools.)*

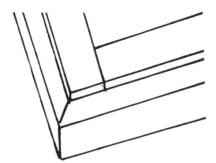

69-11. *Make glass support. (Courtesy of Stanley Tools.)*

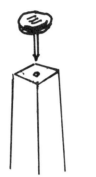

69-12. *Install glides. (Courtesy of Stanley Tools.)*

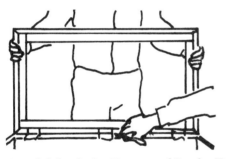

69-13. *Attach lid to body. (Courtesy of Stanley Tools.)*

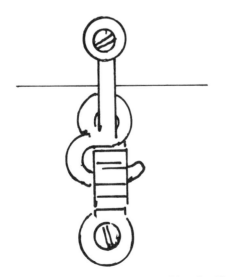

69-14. *Add cabinet hooks. (Courtesy of Stanley Tools.)*

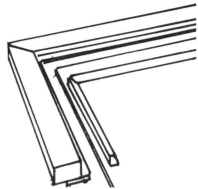

69-15. *Install glass. (Courtesy of Stanley Tools.)*

The bottom panel is ¾″ plywood. T-nuts to match the hanger screws for the legs (most are ⁵⁄₁₆″ × 18 threads) are installed after the bottom panel is cut to 38½″ × 22½″. T-nuts are set in 1¼″ from each edge, in ⅜″ holes. Seat T-nuts with a mallet to keep from damaging the face. Some legs come with metal top plates; there's no need for T-nuts with these. The metal plate is screwed to the underside of the bottom panel. Use only ¾″ screws to attach such a plate, as longer screws will stick through the bottom panel.

From the bottom of the panel, drill pilot holes to take No. 8 × 1¼″ long flathead screws. Place the bottom panel on the sides of table, with a ¼″ inset all around. Mark and drill starter holes, and add glue. Fasten with 1¼″ × No. 8 screws.

The ¼″ × ¾″ screen moulding is fastened with 1″ brads and glue to the exposed plywood edge. Mitre corners. If legs with metal plates are used, change and use 1¼″ wide lattice moulding to hide the plates.

Mitre two pieces of one-by-two flat, and 39″ long. Do the same to two more pieces of one-by-two, 29″ long. Countersink for No. 8 screws. Glue and screw mitres together, keeping the assembly square. Clamp until dry.

To support the glass, cut two pieces of ⁹⁄₃₂″ × 1⅜″ lattice 37¼″ long, and two pieces 18½″ long. Countersink holes for No. 6 screws at 6″ intervals, ⅜″ from the outside edge and ⅜″ from each end of long pieces—¾″ on the short pieces. Place the lattice ⅞″ from the outside edge. Glue and screw with No. 6 × ¾″ screws. Longer lattice pieces extend beyond the mitre to provide support.

Glides are placed in ³⁄₃₂″ starter holes in legs. Screw leg hanger bolts, or plates, to the bottom of the table.

Using the hinges, attach the lid to the body of the table. Hinge barrels extend just beyond the outside edge of the lid; mark and drill starter holes (use an awl to make these small starter holes, if you want). Screw hinges to lid. Mark and drill starter holes in the tabletop rear sides. Attach the lid so all sides are flush.

Brass cabinet hooks are installed 3″ in from each end, and the lid support is added to support the lid.

Finally, fit the ¼″ plate glass in the rabbet made by the lattice. It is held in place with the stop moulding, with 45-degree mitres on the corners. Before attaching the moulding, lift glass out, and make sure all surfaces are sanded smooth with 180 or 200 grit sandpaper. Stain as desired, and coat with felt or other interior material along the inside of the bottom panel. Install stop moulding with the 1″ brads.

70 ♦ Dining–Game Table

This table serves slightly different purposes than the one above. It is a game table, with a top large enough for use as a small dining table. The top insert material is up to you, and will cause some variation in size, thus in the materials list (and, if material such as ceramic tile is used, in the tool list). The materials listed here are for wood parquet tabletops.

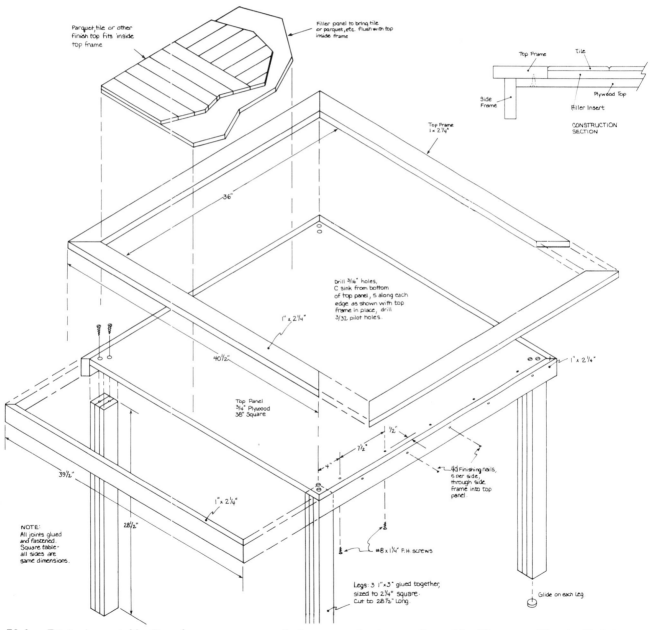

70-1.   *Dining/game table. Procedures are pretty much the same as for the preceding table. (Courtesy of Stanley Tools.)*

Materials

- thirty-six 6″ × 6″ wood parquet
- eight one-by-three × 8′ pine or hardwood (ripped to 2¼″)
- ¾″ plywood, 38″ × 38″
- sixteen ½″ corrugated nails
- No. 8 × 1¼″ and × 2″ flathead Phillips wood screws
- 4d finishing nails
- four metal leg glides
- wood glue
- 120-grit sandpaper

Tools

- circular saw
- finishing sander
- hammer
- nail set
- corrugated nail set
- mitre box and backsaw
- Phillips driver bit
- drill, VSR clutched, 5/16″ brad point drill bit
- square
- measuring tape
- surform
- 4″ C-clamps
- corner clamp
- dowel centers

Check final height of parquet and ¾″ plywood table-top base: any remaining space requires a hardboard or other filler to make sure the parquet is flush with the framing of edges. Check exact dimensions of the parquet, too, as slight differences in sizes require adjustments to the top perimeter size, as well as depth.

Have the lumberyard rip all 3″ (actually about 2½″) stock to 2¼″. Glue up three pieces of the resulting ¾″ × 2¼″ stock to make 2¼″ square material. Cut leg pieces to length, plus 2″ on each end. Sand smooth, clean off, and glue up with C-clamps, making sure all edges are flush. When the glue is dry, scrape off the excess and cut the legs to exact lengths.

Cut the plywood top to size. Make sure, during layout, that all angles are true, and check after cutting. Cut the 2¼″ side stock to a perfect mitre on the mitre box. The side stock is then fastened to the edge of the plywood with glue and 4d nails. Mitre joints may then be reinforced with ½″ corrugated nails, if desired.

Fasten the legs to the bottom of the plywood top with glue and two 2″ No. 8 flathead wood screws. Also glue the legs to the side frame.

Make the top frame so it extends 1¼″ beyond the edge of the plywood top on all four sides. Use the mitre box for accurate cuts, and do the assembly on a flat

surface. Make joints with glue and corrugated fasteners on the underside of the joints. Use a corner clamp to hold joints while fastening. After the glue dries, set the top frame in place and fasten it to the plywood and legs with glue and No. 8 × 1¼″ screws set 8″ apart. Screws must run up through the plywood and into the top frame.

Make any needed adjustment of thickness for the finish top materials. Lay in the parquet with adhesive. Finish as desired, after sanding well with fine sandpaper.

71 ◆ Breadboard

Sometimes called kneading boards, these boards are most often made in poplar, but may be found in pine, cherry, walnut, and other woods. Construction is simple, and reasonably fast.

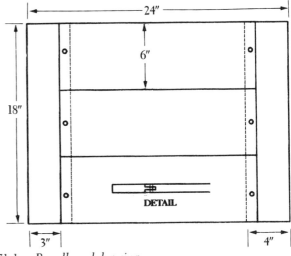

71-1. *Breadboard drawing.*

Materials

- three one-by-six × 18″ poplar
- two one-by-four × 18″ poplar
- six ⅜″ × ¾″ dowels, walnut for contrasting color
- four joiner biscuits
- wood glue
- 120-grit sandpaper
- salad bowl finish

Cut wide poplar boards to 18″ length. Center ¼″ width dado blade on scrap stock the same thickness as the poplar, and then cut slots in the thin poplar, on one edge, with the grain (18″ width). Make the slot at least 1″ deep, but no more than 1½″ deep. (A router with ¼″ and ¾″ straight bits could be used for all of the dado operations.)

Set dado to full-width cut (most are ¹³⁄₁₆″) and cut at exact groove depth for width of tongue, minus ¹⁄₁₆″ for expansions and contraction. Cut tongues on both ends of the wide boards to a light ¼″ thickness, centered so it fits into the end-board slots.

Assemble to check. If all is well, join the wide boards with two biscuits per board. Glue and clamp lightly, making sure the assembly is as flat as possible. Sand lightly to make sure the wide board is flat after the glue dries. Insert tongues into the end boards. Center a walnut dowel in each of wide boards. Glue, let dry, and sand. Do *not* glue the entire tongue assembly, as that will fairly quickly cause splitting of the board with the differing rates of expansion for cross grain and end grain.

Sand with 120-grit paper, and give two or three coats of salad bowl finish. The resulting board can serve for kneading bread, slicing bread, serving items, and in many other ways.

Tools
- table saw, dado blade set
- backsaw
- biscuit joiner
- ¼″ wood chisel
- ¾″ or 1″ wood chisel

6 · Plywood Projects

This chapter is devoted to projects that are *primarily* constructed of plywood. Many of these projects, while easy and quick, are of larger sizes because of the type of work plywood in large panels lends itself to.

72 · Waferboard Desk

I built this desk some years ago, as an oversize unit, for use and for Georgia-Pacific. It is about as low-cost as a desk can get, and would require few changes today, if I were to reconstruct it (but, it's still in use, though the computer in the photo has been traded in since).

Start by cutting all materials to size, then begin assembling the pedestals. These are really simple boxes, with a divider to provide shelf space above the drawer. Sides are of ¾″ material, 24″ deep and 26″ tall. Bottoms and tops are also ¾″ material, 16″ wide and 23½″ deep. Backs are ½″ waferboard, 16″ wide and 24½″ high. Assemble with butt joints, using glue and 4d finishing nails. The bottoms and tops fit inside the sides. The back fits inside the side pieces, and overlaps the bottoms and tops.

Shelf holders are one-by-two × 23½″ long, with shelves of ½″ material, 16″ wide and 23½″ deep. The front is covered with either edging tape or solid-wood edging to make things ready for the drawers. I used 2″ wide pine for edging. Check for square as you go.

72-1. Waferboard desk.

94

Materials

- one and one-half sheets ¾″ waferboard or OSB
- one-half sheet ½″ waferboard or OSB
- 31″ × 97″ plastic laminate
- ¾″ × 12″ × 30″ birch-faced plywood
- three 96″ lengths door-stop moulding
- five 96″ × 1″ × 4″ pine or fir
- one-half sheet ½″ A-C plywood
- two 3½″ drawer pulls
- 4d finishing nails
- twenty 2½″ × No. 8 drive screws
- twelve 1¼″ × No. 8 drive screws
- two 24″ wood drawer glide sets
- contact cement
- 100-grit sandpaper
- wood filler
- stain
- tung oil

Tools

- circular saw (carbide-tipped blade)
- saw guide or 8′ straightedge and clamps
- four 4′ bar or pipe clamps
- router, ¼″ and ½″ straight bits, ⅜″ rabbetting bit
- edge guide
- hammer
- drill, Phillips driver bit, ³⁄₃₂″ drill bit
- mallet
- measuring tape
- square
- chisel

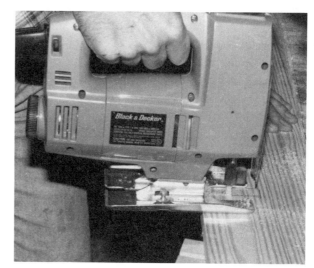

72-3. *Cutting shelf holders.*

Drawer fronts are of particle board core birch plywood, 11″ high and 15″ wide. The drawer has ½″ sanded plywood sides and ¼″ hardboard for the bottom. All assembly is done with 4d nails and glue.

The drawer front is rabbeted to fit the front moulding used, with the rabbet set ½″ deep and as wide as needed. The drawer front needs ½″ dadoes cut to hold the sides, and the drawer bottom is held in ¼″ grooves. Dadoes for the drawer back are cut 1″ in from the back edges of the sides to provide enough strength. Drawer sides are 10″, tapering to 7″ at the 4″ mark on both front and back.

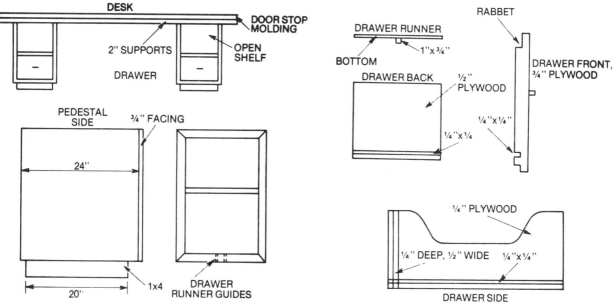

72-2. *Desk drawing. (Courtesy of Georgia-Pacific Corporation.)*

To vary the desk height, change the width of the toe boards under the pedestals. I made mine of one-by-fours, which add 3½″ to overall desk height. Toe boards as low as one-by-two and as high as one-by-six are acceptable in appearance, giving a 4″ high variation with no real work or expense. Assemblies are 20″ deep by 15″ wide, which requires two 18½″ one-by-fours and four 15″ one-by-fours (two are placed in the inside upper ends to provide easy installation, and bracing). Assemble with 1¼″ screws.

72-4.   *Ripping top.*

The top is a simple assembly, with the board ripped to 31″ × 97″. Coat with contact cement, following manufacturer's directions, and install the plastic laminate.

At the time I made the desk, I had no laminate trimming bits, so used a fine-toothed, carbide-tipped saw to cut to final size of 30″ × 96″. The cut lines were first covered with 2″ wide masking tape, and the cut guide was used; the top face was turned down, of course.

Assemble the rest of the top using 2″ edging (I used redwood because it was on hand), and door-stop moulding, with 4d finishing nails and glue. The moulding is mitred and clamped in place.

I finished with rosewood stain, and wiped on several coats of tung oil. That has survived years of intensive use.

73 ◆ Stacking Bookcases

This bookcase project is another that may prove exceptionally handy from time to time. Books are my basic problem when it comes to storage, so I appreciate the ease with which these units went together.

Materials
- two 4′ × 8′ × ¾″ birch-faced plywood sheets
- seven one-by-six × 6′ pine
- No. 8 × 1½″ flathead wood screws
- wood glue
- 120-grit sandpaper
- wood filler
- stain and clear finish

Tools
- circular or table saw
- router, ¾″ straight bit
- edge guide
- jigsaw, 14-tooth jigsaw blades
- pad sander
- belt sander, 100 grit belt
- screwdriver
- drill

73-1.   *Stacking bookcases.*

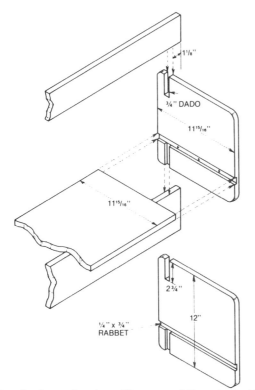

73-2. *Bookcase drawing. (Courtesy of Georgia-Pacific Corporation.)*

73-3. *Stacking bookcases.*

The materials listed will provide 12 shelf units.

Start by cutting the sides to size ($12'' \times 11^{15}/_{16}''$). Cut dadoes on the sides, making sure you get mirror images. Repeat the process for the slots, again making sure of mirror images.

Cut shelving to size: $11^{15}/_{16}'' \times 31^{3}/_{4}''$. Cut one-by-six backer boards to 34" lengths.

Once all of the parts are cut, use a jigsaw to cut round corners, with a 1" radius. Smooth those with a belt sander, as needed. Assemble the units and check fits. If fits are okay, disassemble, and lay the pieces out for staining. The original unit had no edge treatment other than extra coats of finish.

74 ✦ Stackable Beds

These units are real space savers, making sure there is room for the unexpected guest, no matter how crowded you are already.

74-1. *Stacking beds. (Courtesy of Georgia-Pacific Corporation.)*

Materials
- one and one-half sheets 4' × 8' × ¾" A-A interior plywood
- two 4' × 8' × ⅝" A-B or A-C sanded plywood
- six two-by-two × 8' pine or fir
- two 39" × 75" foam mattresses
- paint
- wood filler
- 100-grit sandpaper
- wood glue
- 6d finishing nails
- 4d finishing nails

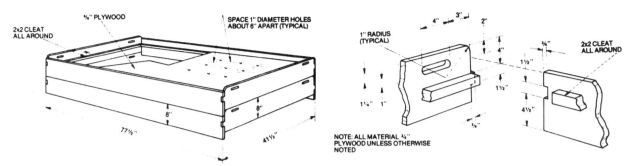

74-2. *Bed drawing. (Courtesy of Georgia-Pacific Corporation.)*

Tools

- table saw, or circular saw and guide
- drill, 1″ spade bit
- jigsaw
- compass or trammel points
- hammer
- nail set
- square
- measuring tape

You can use a circular saw to cut plywood to the correct widths, if no table saw is available, or have it custom-cut.

Carefully measure and mark cutouts to be made in bed's sides, then drill starting holes at each end of the slots with the 1″ bit. A spade bit is a rough working tool, so you must back the wood up tightly (clamped) with another piece of wood to prevent bad tear-out. Join the holes with the jigsaw.

Sand all pieces and glue and nail the sides and ends together, using 4d finishing nails. Cut two-by-two cleats to support mattresses to run the length of each side and end. Glue and nail the cleats in place with 6d finishing nails.

Place the ⅝″ mattress support board on top of the cleats, and nail it in place, using 4d finishing nails spaced every 6″. To save time, you can use 1″ drive screws spaced at 1′ intervals. This also provides a stronger joint.

Drill 1″ holes at 6″ spacing in the plywood bottom so air can reach the mattress. Sand and paint. With mattresses added, the beds are ready to be used and stacked.

75 ♦ Workbench

Like many of my projects, this workbench is oversize. Overall length is 97½″, and depth is 30″. It is easy to construct, and lasts well.

Materials

- ¾″ OSB or waferboard
- one-half sheet ½″ A-C sanded plywood
- 24″ × 96″ × ¼″ hardboard
- two one-by-six × 8′ pine
- one one-by-six × 48″
- four one-by-four × 8′
- two pairs overlay hinges
- 1¼″ and 2″ drive screws
- two 3½″ × ¼″ carriage bolts, washers, nuts
- sixteen 2¾″ or 3″ × ¼″ carriage bolts, washers, nuts
- 4d finishing nails
- ten 2″ × ¼″ lag screws
- 100-grit sandpaper

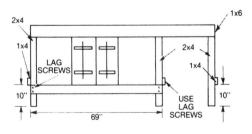

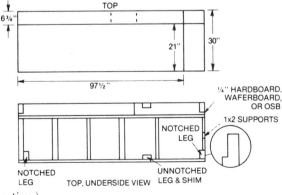

75-1. *Workbench drawing. (Courtesy of Georgia-Pacific Corporation.)*

Tools

- circular saw
- saw guide (or 8′ straightedge) and clamps
- hammer
- screwdriver bits
- drill, clutched, ⅛″, ¼″, ³⁄₁₆″ drill bits
- ⁷⁄₁₆″ and ½″ wrench
- wood rasp

Start by cutting the ¾″ OSB or waferboard to size, 21″ × 96″. Place the best face of the material on a flat surface, and use three straight pieces of one-by-six sheathing board for the front, back, and tool tray divider. Square lumber ends at 96″ long. Cut two 30″ end pieces of one-by-six.

Using the 2″ drive screws, assemble the basic box using glue as well. Use three or four screws per joint, and assemble the tool tray divider and front inside the two ends first. Then add the back one-by-six.

Cut four pieces of one-by-four to 21″ lengths. Set these on top of the in-place waferboard, and attach to the frame sides with 1¼″ screws and glue.

Cut three legs to 34″ lengths, and three to 33⅛″ lengths. The long legs fit in back, where there is no top. Two legs on each of the back and the front fit with the long sides along the bench ends, and the center legs fit with the long side along the long boards. The two outside front legs must be notched over the front supports. The center front leg is not notched, but needs a shim of the same stock used for top supports, so it needs the long (3½″) carriage bolts, instead of the 3″ or 2¾″ used in the other legs.

75-3.   *Cutting workbench top.*

Attach legs loosely to frame. Cut leg braces from one-by-fours. One is 69″ long, three 29″ long, and one 96″ long. The longest brace is attached first, to the back legs, with the top of the brace 10″ above the bottoms of the legs. Mark and clamp the braces on the legs while drilling for carriage bolts and screws. Drill lag screw pilot holes only about one-half to two-thirds the depth of the screw. Carriage bolt holes always go all the way through. Finally, tighten all bolts and braces while making sure all corners remain square.

Place two dividers in the tool tray, each 6″ × 5½″. Use 4d finishing nails and glue. Set the workbench on its legs, leaving the top on the floor for the moment.

75-2.   *Workbench.*

75-4. *Clamp, then drill and bolt legs in place.*

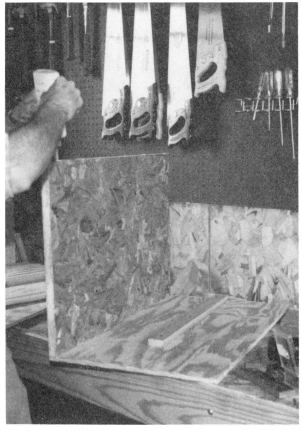

75-5. *Assembling the cabinet.*

Cut three waferboard shelves, each 30″ deep, with two 21″ wide and one 19″ wide. The 19″ piece is the cabinet bottom. Install the 21″ shelves using three 2″ drive screws at front and three at the back of each. Notch board ends to fit around nuts and bolts, as needed.

The center space takes a cabinet 21″ wide with no difficulty. Make sides heights at least ⅜″ shorter than the bottom of the front rail of the bench top. This will allow ⅛″ clearance under the tool tray in back.

Sides and top are cut from ½″ A-C plywood, as is a 17¾″ shelf. Cut the back 18″ wide × 17½″ high from the same wood. Assemble back, bottom, and sides with 4d finishing nails and glue. Cut two 24″ one-by-two cleats and install them as shelf supports inside the cabinet. Attach from the inside with 1″ screws and glue. Install the top, and insert the finished unit in the workbench, attaching at front and back with 2″ screws, three per frame rail.

Make cabinet doors from one-by-sixes, 18″ long, using two per door. Attach one-by-two cleats with 1¼″ screws, and bevel cleat and door edges. Install with hinges. Touch up any rough edges with a wood rasp.

76, 77, 78 ♦ Patio Table, Chairs, and Lazy Susan

These three projects show how easily plywood can be used to provide outdoor amenities.

76, 77, 78-1. *Patio table, chairs, and Lazy Susan. (Courtesy of the American Plywood Association.)*

Start by laying the parts out on the panels, as shown in the drawings. Use a compass to make corner radii. Make sure all lines allow for the 1/8″ kerf your saw blade will remove.

Cut parts and remove rough edges.

Start assembling the table with the leg assembly as shown going on the tabletop. Go from there to the lazy Susan, which is a useful item to have.

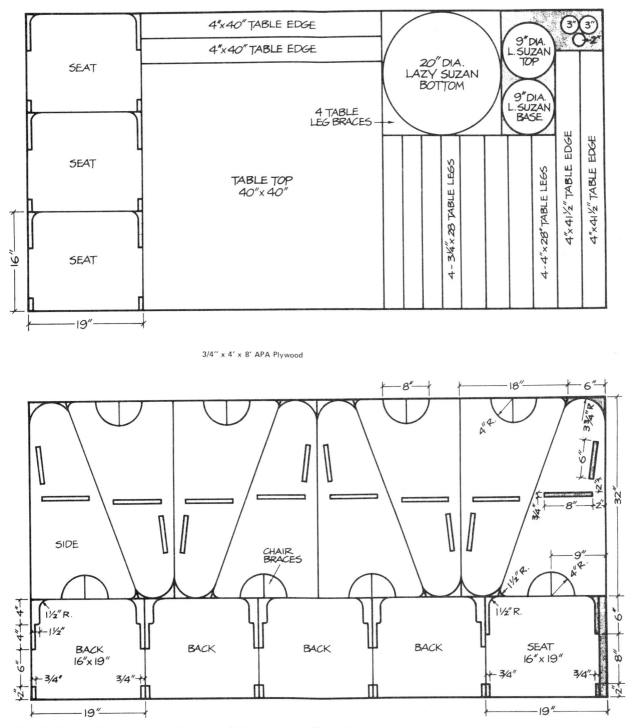

76, 77, 78-2.   *Panel layout. (Courtesy of the American Plywood Association.)*

Materials

- two ¾″ × 48″ × 96″ medium-density overlay plywood
- eight 1¼″ round-head wood screws
- ⅜″ × 3″ dowel (for lazy Susan)
- 6″ diameter bearing (for lazy Susan)
- lb. 6d galvanized finishing nails
- urea resin glue
- wood filler
- sandpaper
- paint

Tools

- circular saw
- square
- measuring tape
- hammer
- nail set
- paint brush
- pad sander
- compass

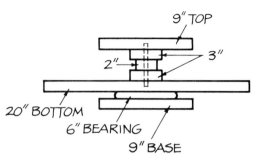

76, 77, 78-4.   *Lazy Susan drawing. (Courtesy of the American Plywood Association.)*

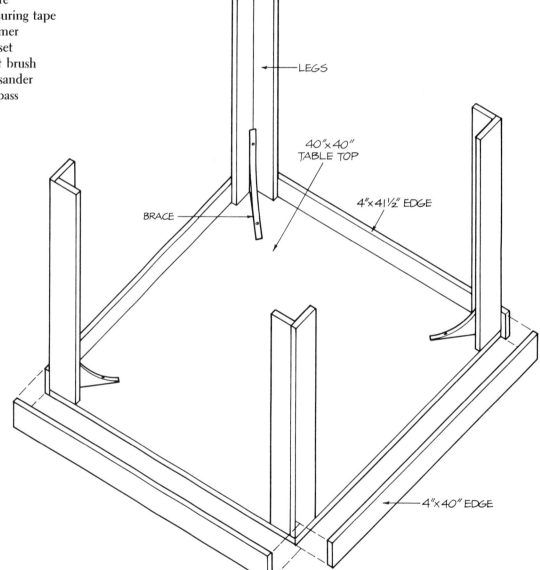

76, 77, 78-3.   *Leg assembly drawing. (Courtesy of the American Plywood Association.)*

Assemble chairs next. Urea resin glue provides a water-resistant setup. A good coat of latex paint also helps preserve the projects through much outdoor use.

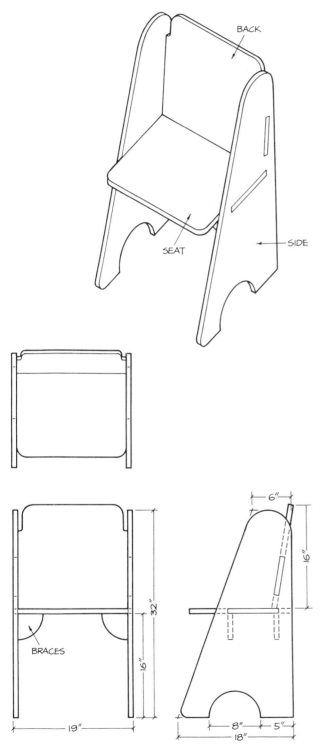

76, 77, 78-5. *Chair assembly. (Courtesy of the American Plywood Association.)*

79 ◆ Toy Box Bench

Toys are the bane of many a parent's existence: children have access to more toys of more types than ever before, and most parents seem to buy as many as they can possibly afford. Toys, toys, toys—scattered all over the place. This toy box bench provides storage space, and a place to sit and ponder during the child's quieter times.

79-1. *Toy box bench. (Courtesy of the American Plywood Association.)*

Materials
• ½" × 4' × 4' medium-density overlay plywood (both sides MDO)
• plastic laminate, 41" × 25½"
• 41" long piano hinge, with screws
• four rubber bumpers
• six No. 6 × 1" round-head wood screws
• contact cement
• 100-grit sandpaper
• enamel and primer

Tools
• circular saw
• jigsaw
• drill, ⅛", ½" drill bit
• screwdriver
• paint brush
• mallet
• square
• measuring tape
• compass or trammel points and bar

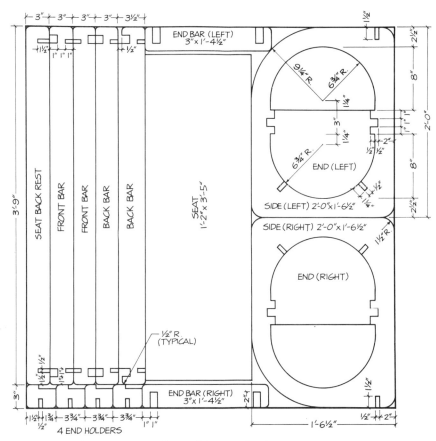

79-2. *Panel layout. (Courtesy of the American Plywood Association.)*

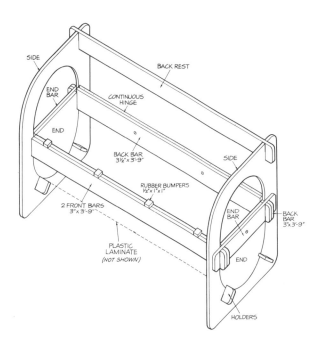

79-3. *Bench drawing. (Courtesy of the American Plywood Association.)*

Cut the plywood to the dimensions shown in the layout, and smooth the edges.

Drill pilot holes and screw the end pieces together, after which screw the piano hinge to the lid and one back bar.

Drill screw pass holes in the plastic laminate, then heat the laminate (a tub of hot water does fine) until it's flexible, and sandwich the edges between the two front bars and the two back bars, letting it curve up underneath. Fasten with wood screws.

Assemble the ends, end supports, and the seat backrest. Install seat bumpers, tape off the laminate and bumpers, and paint the remainder.

80 ◆ Firewood Storage Carrier

Keeping the home fire burning can be pleasant, and sometimes fun, but it can be a pain to lug the firewood around, and to store it indoors. This box reduces these problems, and is very easy to build.

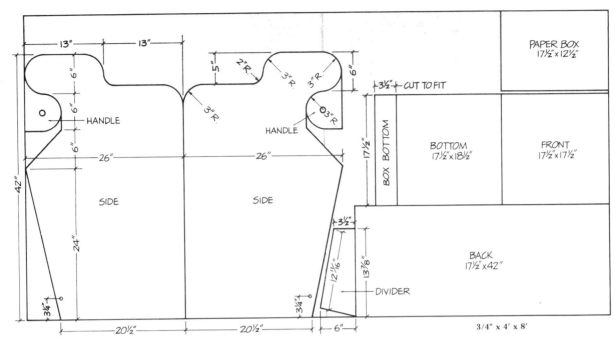

80-1. *Panel layout. (Courtesy of the American Plywood Association.)*

Materials

- ¾" × 4' × 8' medium-density overlay plywood, overlaid both sides (or A-B interior plywood)
- 1" × 17½" wood dowel
- two 7" wheels, with nuts and washers
- 24" threaded axle rod
- two angle irons
- 6d finishing nails
- wood glue
- latex paint
- eight ¾" × No. 10 wood screws to hold angle iron in place

Tools

- circular saw
- jigsaw
- drill, ⅛" bit, ½" and ¼" bits for metal
- wood rasp
- paint brush
- screwdriver

Cut the parts to size as shown on the layout sheet. When laying out, make sure to leave enough room for kerfs during cutting.

Assemble the back inside the sides first, then add the bottom, and the front, using 6d finishing nails and glue for all fastening. Set all nails.

Position and add the divider in the rear compartment, then add the box wall. Finally, add the back box bottom. Again, use 6d finishing nails and glue.

80-2. *Firewood storage box. (Courtesy of the American Plywood Association.)*

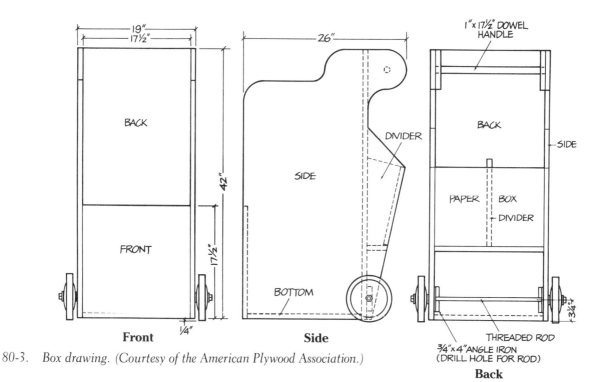

Front ¼" **Side**

80-3. *Box drawing. (Courtesy of the American Plywood Association.)*

Back

Holes for the axle are ½" diameter and are backed with angle irons drilled for the axle and screwed onto the underside of the box. Make sure the axle midline is no more than 3¼" above the bottom of the box. If much outdoor use is expected, drop the axle line 1" (to 2¼") for increased wheel clearance. You can also add two screwed-on 3" long × 2" wide × ¾" pieces in front, with one on each side, and each being 1" lower than the actual bottom of the box. This will help prevent front-ward tilts during indoor use, but still allow plenty of clearance outdoors.

81, 82, 83 ◆ Computer Desk and Wall Units

Computers may be very helpful tools, but they do require different, and more, desk space. These designs use hardwood-faced plywood to provide an efficient, and attractive, working space.

Tools
- circular saw
- saw guide
- router, ¼" straight bit
- edge guide
- hammer
- nail set
- drill, assorted bits
- iron or veneer tape press
- screwdriver
- pad sander

81, 82, 83-1. *Computer desk. (Courtesy of Georgia-Pacific Corporation.)*

Materials

(for all three projects)
- 4' × 8' × ¾" hardwood plywood
- two one-by-two × 48" pine, or fir
- two fixed casters, 2" diameter
- two rotating casters, 2" diameter
- ¼" × 48" × 48" hardboard
- two wood drawer guides, 23¼" long
- pin-style shelf clips
- 8d, 6d, 4d finishing nails
- 50' iron-on veneer tape to match plywood
- two drawer pulls
- wood glue
- wood filler
- stain
- polyurethane finish
- 150-grit sandpaper

Start by drawing the parts at exact size on the back side of the plywood. Most cuts will be made from the back side when using a circular saw—the saw splinters most on the *up* side of the wood, so the good side is placed down. You can reduce splintering by covering the cut lines with masking tape (mark again over the tape, of course).

Cut all pieces, and mitre the edges. If you are going to use edging tape, I would suggest forgetting mitring the edges.

For the keyboard unit, cut those pieces first. Attach the sides and back using glue and nails. Glue and nail

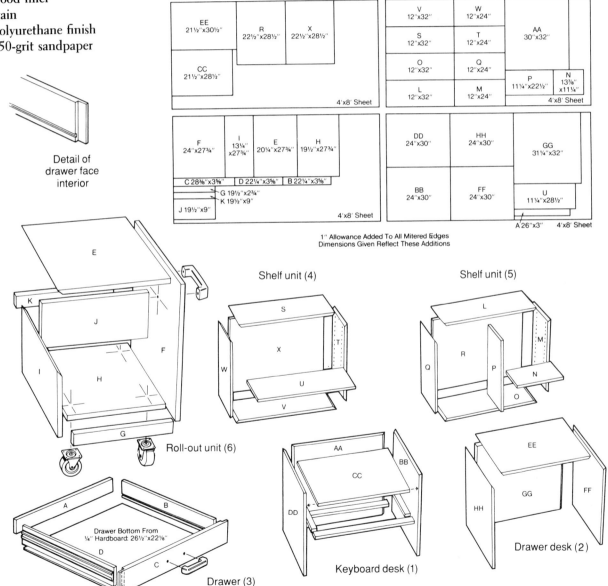

81, 82, 83-2. *Desk drawing. (Courtesy of Georgia-Pacific Corporation.)*

one-by-two cleats to the back and sides of the desk to support the top. Next, glue and nail a one-by-two face rail to the underside of the desktop. Apply glue to the top of the cleats and place the desk surface on the cleats. Drive 4d nails up through the cleats and into the underside of the desk. Always use the shortest possible nail to reduce chances of over-penetration.

For the drawer desk, cut out the pieces and butt the edges. Assemble the sides, back, and top. Attach the drawer guide to the inside surface, as directed by the manufacturer.

The drawer is now built, with ¾″ plywood for the front, and a ¼″ hardwood bottom. The drawings show metal hardware on the sides, but the hardware suggested is center-mounted bottom, and easier to use, without messing up any drawers.

Make the drawer as shown, with dadoes ¼″ wide and ⅜″ deep routed in sides and front to accept the bottom. Attach the drawer pull and insert the drawer.

The roll-out unit takes a bit more time, and uses the 2″ casters listed. The dimensions presented will fit the largest printers available, including many laser units with overhanging feed trays. You may alter the depth as you desire to fit smaller printers, but the extra space is probably going to get used for something, possibly ribbon or cartridge storage.

Cut pieces after drawing them on the plywood, doing the cutting as described above. Mount the bottom opening support at least 12″ from the edge that will face the chair, preferably 18″. This support is needed to provide structural rigidity, but it also must be mounted in such a way to allow decent storage.

Assemble bottom inside sides, and top over sides, with the inside support and other supports nailed in place as shown. Place the casters at or near the corners, and position the drawer pull. Do not install hardware just yet, though you may drill required holes.

Finish all the desk pieces by sanding with 150 grit sandpaper, and staining, if desired, and then coating with polyurethane.

Now come the wall units that make the computer desk able to have clear desk space for other uses. The larger wall unit gets the monitor up off the desk.

Mark and cut as shown for the two shelf units. Drill end parts for shelf-support pins where needed—this means, drill the inside of one end piece on one shelf unit, and the right side of one center piece to face that. On the other unit, drill the insides of both ends. (I suggest lining up the center spots for drilling these ¼″ holes to accept shelf-support pins by using a piece of pegboard. Use spring or C-clamps to make sure it stays where you want it. Mark the holes to be drilled with white-out or some similar substance, spacing them 2″ or more apart.)

Assemble with glue and 6d nails, with top and bottom overlapping sides. Apply edge tape. Sand lightly, stain and finish.

When hanging these wall units, it is imperative that you use enough fasteners, and strike studs, or use the best hollow wall fasteners going. Make sure the wall units are going to stay on the walls, no matter the weight applied. That's the reason the backing boards on these units are of ¾″ material, whereas most shelf projects use ¼″ backing boards to save cost and weight.

84 ◆ Storage Headboard

This project is large, but easy, and fun to make, while adding a great deal to storage space in any bedroom. The size is variable, depending on the width of your bed, so materials listings may be adjusted, though the measurements shown will come close to fitting most beds and rooms.

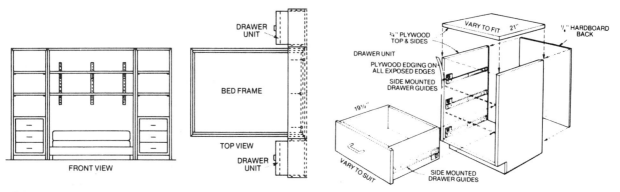

84-1.   *Headboard drawing. (Courtesy of Georgia-Pacific Corporation.)*

Materials

- five ¾″ × 4′ × 8′ A-A or A-B plywood
- ½″ × 4′ × 8′ A-A or A-B sanded plywood
- 150′ edge tape
- four one-by-ten × 8′ pine (use one-by-twelve for deeper shelves)
- six drawer slides
- four 48″ shelf standards
- eighteen 10″ (or 12″) shelf supports
- sixteen pin-style shelf supports
- 6d, 4d, 2d finishing nails
- wood glue
- six drawer knobs or handles
- paint
- 120-grit sandpaper

Tools

- circular saw
- saw guide
- router, ½″, ¾″ straight bits, ¼″ rabbetting bit
- edge guide
- drill, ⅛″ pilot bit, ¼″ brad point bit
- drill depth stop
- hammer
- nail set
- heavy-duty metal snips
- hacksaw with 18 t.p.i. blade
- fine file
- pad sander
- paint brushes

Start by measuring your bed. Most double beds are 54″ wide, with queen-size units measuring 60″. King-size beds are 72″ or 76″ wide. Add on allowances for sheets and other bedding, plus some space for the hands that have to make the bed. Make all clearances at least 1½″.

Make the end shelf units first, using ¾″ plywood for the sides, top, and inside divider. The units are at least 20″ wide, and as deep as you wish the shelves to be. Measure in ⅜″ from each back edge and rout in a dado ¼″ deep and ½″ wide down one side of each piece (four

84-2.   Storage headboard. (Courtesy of Georgia-Pacific Corporation.)

pieces). Cut a panel to fit the back of the unit, using the ½" plywood. Rabbet the top edges ¾" wide by ½" deep to accept the top. Use edging tape on all exposed edges.

For adjustable shelves, you can use a piece of pegboard (mentioned in the previous set of projects) and mark off the drill 7⁄16" deep by ¼" holes for the pins (depth of hole is after penetration of the pegboard). Cut shelves to fit, making them about 3⁄8" shorter than the actual space. Assemble the units with 4d and 6d nails and glue.

The center shelves are much wider than the end shelves, but generally go up in much the same manner. Because they're wider, different shelf-support systems are needed. Assemble with 4d and 6d finishing nails, and glue. Use edging tape on edges.

Use a ¾" backing board here, and install three standard-style shelf supports, which usually come with their own Phillips head screws, about 1" long. Nip the ends off the shelf-support flags so they don't curl up in front of the shelves.

Drawer units shown are 19½" deep and 28" high, good general sizes. Drawers that go too deep aren't a good idea, but the height and width are readily adjusted. As sized, three drawers per unit work well.

Cut two panels for each unit, 19½" × 27½" high. Make toe space cutouts 3" to 3½" high. Bottom panels are cut 19½" to the appropriate width. The top is 1½" wider than the bottom, with the same 19½" depth. Rabbet the backs of the sides, tops, and bottoms to accept a ¼" hardboard back.

You may butt-joint drawers all around, but setting in a dado groove for the ¼" bottom provides for sturdier construction. Sides may also be dadoed into the front, and the back into the sides—all of which *adds* the depth of the dadoes to the lengths of material required. Never dado more than half the depth of the wood being cut for this sort of work. Assemble the drawers with 2d and 4d finishing nails and glue.

Use plywood edging tape to cover raw edges. Place assembled units together to check fits, and make sure all units are flush. They may then be screwed together with No. 8 × 1¼" wood screws, about ¼" in from the edges, to form a single unit. I would suggest painting *after* screwing the units together, which means not having to paint hidden raw wood.

---

85 ◆ Trash Bin

For those who don't need protection added for firewood (Project 18), this bin for trash cans helps keep the house and lawn neat-looking.

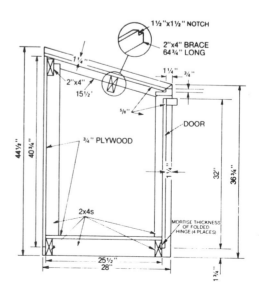

85-1.   *Trash bin. (Courtesy of Georgia-Pacific Corporation.)*

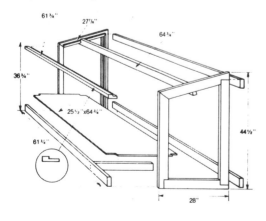

85-2.   *Bin drawing. (Courtesy of Georgia-Pacific Corporation.)*

Materials

- two ⅝″ × 4′ × 8′ T1-11 siding, 4″ on center
- one and one-half ¾″ × 4′ × 8′ B-B sanded exterior plywood
- eleven two-by-four × 6′ pine or fir
- four 4″ × 4″ hinges, with screws
- two double roller catches, with springs
- construction adhesive
- 4d, 8d galvanized finishing nails
- paint

Tools

- circular saw
- router, ¾″ straight bit
- router edge guide
- handsaw
- tape measure
- hammer
- square
- wood chisel, ¾″
- screwdriver
- nail set

Cut the two-by-fours for side frames to the sizes in the drawing, and assemble with construction adhesive and 8d finishing nails. Rabbet the top front brace as shown (1¼″ × ¾″ deep), using the router, straight bit, and edge guide. Two passes on a table-saw dado blade will also do the job. Cut all braces to length and attach to the side frames with construction adhesive and 8d nails. Use the handsaw to notch the top center brace to accept a two-by-four (notch of 1½″ × 1½″).

With framing up, plan the cuts for the siding. You want to cut with the good side down, unless you're using a table saw. Cut the material, and then attach one-by-two cleats to the sides with construction adhesive and 8d finishing nails. Install the roof and side pieces with adhesive and 4d finishing nails.

The back and floor sections are cut from the ¾″ plywood—you might wish to use treated plywood for these parts, and particularly for the floor. Cut 2″ × 3″ notches, with the handsaw, at the corners of the plywood piece for the floor. Rip the front handgrip from a two-by-four. Glue and nail the two-by-four cross-brace for the spot where the two pieces of plywood meet. Then, install the floor, with construction adhesive and 4d nails.

The plywood back panel is 40¾″ × 61¾″, glued and nailed, with 4d nails, in place. Glue and nail the handgrip to the door. Using the chisel, mortise in the hinges in the lower front brace. Make the mortise the depth of the hinge. Stain or paint the bin to suit your home, and then install the catches and the hinges.

86 ◆ Rolling Tool Stand

This all-plywood saw stand can be altered to suit nearly any tool with a base size no larger than my sliding table saw (roughly 20″ square). It moves easily, and carries plenty of extra blades and other accessories.

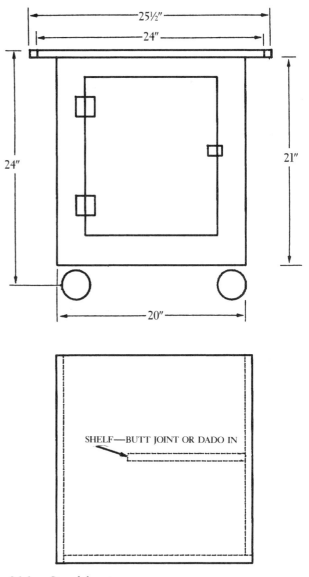

86-1. Stand drawing.

Materials

- ¾″ × 4′ × 8′ B-C interior sanded plywood
- ½″ × 2′ × 2′ B-C interior sanded plywood
- four ¾″ × 3″ × 24″ fir or pine
- ¾″ × ¾″ × 12′ pine
- four ¾″ × 4′ × 4′ B-C plywood

- two 2½″ × 1¾″ brass hinges
- one cupboard catch
- four lockable, swivelling 3″ casters, plus screws
- 4d finishing nails
- eight 1½″ × No. 6 drive screws
- wood glue
- spray paint

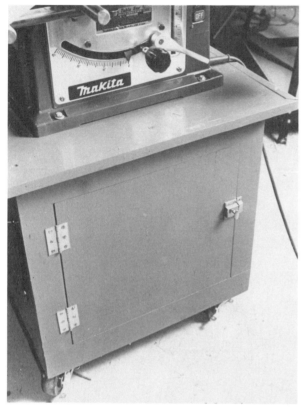

86-2. *Rolling tool stand.*

Start by cutting all pieces to the following sizes: (all of ¾″ material) two sides 20″ × 21″ high; front door 16″ × 18″; back 21″ × 21½″; bottom 21¾″ × 22¼″; top 24″ square. Inside shelf is cut 16″ deep × 22¼″ wide of ½″ material, to fit into a dado cut about halfway up in each side. I didn't cut a dado in the inside back, but you may if you wish. I used a ¾″ × ¾″ cleat to provide support there, though the cabinet is so overbuilt that no further support is really needed. Cut the ¾″ × ¾″ strips to fit the edges of the top, mitre, and attach with 4d nails and glue.

Assemble the basic box (after cutting dadoes around the bottom and the shelf) using 4d finishing nails and glue. Keep checking for square as you go. Make a face frame with butted joints of the one-by-three pieces, cutting to measured fit.

Tools
- table or circular saw
- router, ½″ straight bit
- edge guide
- drill, ⅛″ bit
- four 24″ bar clamps, or eight edge clamps
- screwdriver
- hammer
- nail set
- measuring tape
- square

Add the top, centering it over the sides, and attaching, from the top, with drive screws, after drilling pilot holes. Use two screws per side.

Measure the door for fit, and trim if needed. Fill the door edges with wood filler. Paint. Attach hinges, and add the cupboard catch.

87 ◆ Chair with Pullout Stool

This easy-to-make plywood project requires only half a sheet of medium-density overlay plywood (both sides overlaid), or sanded A-B plywood. It takes barely a couple of hours to make.

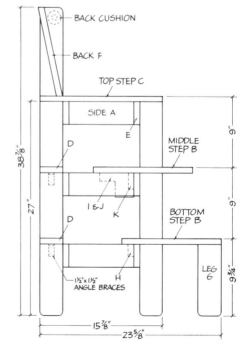

87-1. *Side view. (Courtesy of the American Plywood Association.)*

Lay out the patterns on the half sheet of plywood, on the B side if A-B is used. Cut pieces to size, making slots just a bit oversize to allow for the paint thickness. Make backrest notches 5¾" long, and all the rest 1½" long. To install the backrest, drill holes ½" deep in parts A, both left and right, and glue in the dowel ends. The tube then fits over the 1" of the dowels that extends from each hole.

Materials

- ¾" × 4' × 4' MDO or A-B sanded plywood
- eight 2" No. 8 flathead wood screws
- eight 1" No. 8 flathead wood screws
- four 1½" × No. 8 flathead wood screws
- four 1½" corner braces
- wood glue
- dowels to fill screw holes
- paint
- 120-grit sandpaper
- foam pipe insulation, 12½" × ¾" inside diameter
- shredded foam rubber to fill the tube
- two ⅝" dowels, 1½" long
- four-ply packcloth cover for tube

Finish assembling as shown, sand, and coat with a good-quality latex paint.

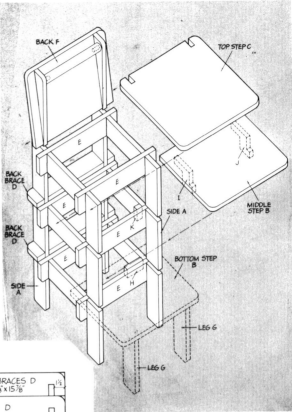

87-3. *Chair and pullout stool. (Courtesy of the American Plywood Association.)*

Tools

- circular saw
- jigsaw
- screwdriver
- drill, ⅝" drill bit
- utility knife
- scissors
- paint brush

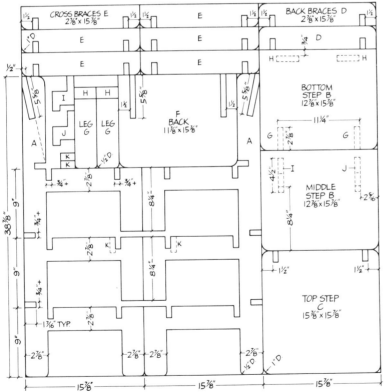

87-2. *Panel layout. (Courtesy of the American Plywood Association.)*

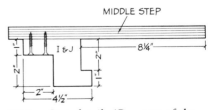

87-4. *Step detail. (Courtesy of the American Plywood Association.)*

88 ◆ Storage Cubes

This is a project for the "old-fashioned" among us; the cubes were originally built to hold LP record albums, but now they serve mostly to hold large books and some magazines. It is all plywood, and very simple to construct using a table saw or router.

Materials
(for each cube)
- two 22″ × 16″ × ½″ A-B plywood
- two 20″ × 16″ × ½″ A-B plywood
- 20″ × 20″ × ½″ A-C plywood (bottom)
- wood glue
- 2d nails
- 100-grit sandpaper
- paint

Tools
- table saw, dado set
- router, ¼″ straight bit
- edge guide
- hammer
- square
- measuring tape
- finishing sander

88-2.   Storage cubes.

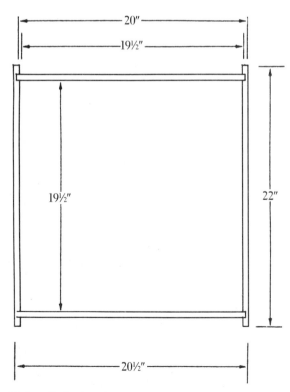

88-1.   Cube drawing.

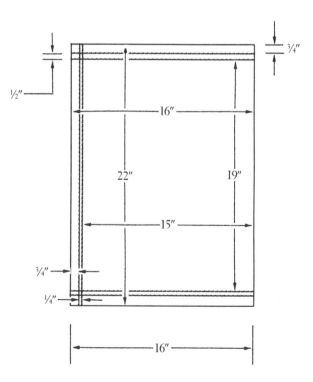

114

Start by cutting all pieces to size. If you're making multiples, I suggest marking out different widths on the plywood to see which arrangement works best. Make cuts with the good face up, on a table saw. Set dado depth to ¼", ¾" from board edge. Make dado passes as indicated on the drawings.

Do any needed cleanup, and insert the bottoms for a dry-fit test. If all is well, assemble using glue and 2d nails. Let the glue dry, sand, and paint.

89 ◆ Armoire

These things were called wardrobes at one time, but now they're armoires. Actually, some of the possible applications of this project have nothing to do with wardrobes, so maybe armoire is right for them. The whole thing begins with a basic box.

Materials
- four ¾" × 4' × 8' A-A plywood
- ¼" × 4' × 8' A-C plywood
- two-by-two × 6'

- ten feet 2¾" crown moulding
- thirty-two feet 1⅛" band moulding
- ten feet ¾" cove moulding
- four ⁵⁄₁₆" T-nuts
- four ⁵⁄₁₆" × 3" hanger bolts
- six 1½" wraparound hinges
- eight 60" shelf standards
- thirty-six shelf clips
- four cushion glides, 1¼"
- twenty-four No. 8 × 1¼" Phillips flathead wood screws (for cleats)
- twelve No. 8 × 2" Phillips flathead wood screws (for shelf supports)
- 8d finishing nails
- 4d finishing nails
- 1" No. 16 brads
- 1¼" box nails
- wood glue
- wood filler
- 80- and 100-grit sandpaper
- sixty feet ¹³⁄₁₆" iron-on edging
- four magnetic catches
- two doorknobs

89-1.   *Wardrobe. (Courtesy of Stanley Tools.)*

89-2.   *Office armoire. (Courtesy of Stanley Tools.)*

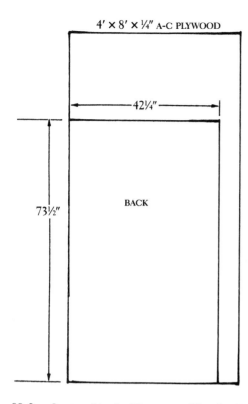

4' × 8' × ¼" A-C PLYWOOD

42¼"

BACK

73½"

89-3. *Layout No. 1. (Courtesy of Stanley Tools.)*

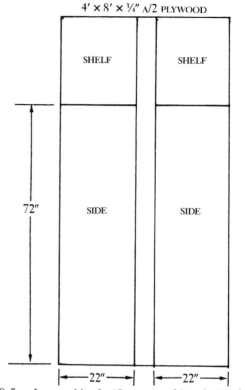

4' × 8' × ¾" A/2 PLYWOOD

SHELF   SHELF

SIDE   SIDE

72"

22"   22"

89-5. *Layout No. 3. (Courtesy of Stanley Tools.)*

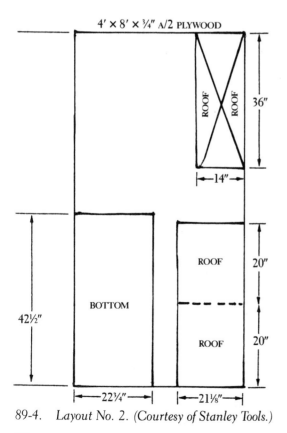

4' × 8' × ¾" A/2 PLYWOOD

ROOF   ROOF

36"

14"

ROOF

20"

BOTTOM

ROOF

20"

42½"

22¾"   21⅛"

89-4. *Layout No. 2. (Courtesy of Stanley Tools.)*

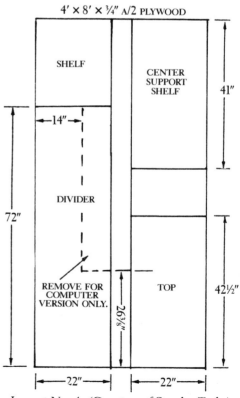

4' × 8' × ¾" A/2 PLYWOOD

SHELF

CENTER
SUPPORT
SHELF

41"

14"

DIVIDER

72"

REMOVE FOR
COMPUTER
VERSION ONLY.

TOP

26⅜"

42½"

22"   22"

89-6. *Layout No. 4. (Courtesy of Stanley Tools.)*

116

Tools

- ½″ and ¾″ wood chisels
- handsaw
- hammer
- nail set
- backsaw and mitre box
- coping saw
- dovetail saw
- measuring tape
- square
- screwdrivers
- drill, with clutch, VSR, No. 2 Phillips power-drive bit, ⅜″ powerbore bit
- various wood bits
- utility knife
- adjustable wrench
- four C-clamps

As a starting suggestion, to keep any of these armoire projects in the easy range, ask your lumber supplier to make all the major cuts on the plywood for you. If they charge, just have them make the rip cuts, and make the crosscuts yourself, at home, using a circular saw and edge guide.

When all of the cuts of the basic box parts are done, drill four ⅜″ holes in the bottom panel, as shown. Using

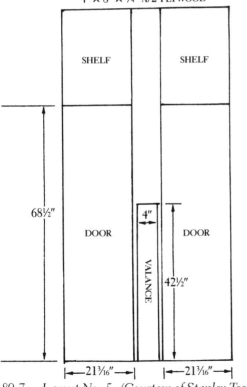

89-7.   *Layout No. 5. (Courtesy of Stanley Tools.)*

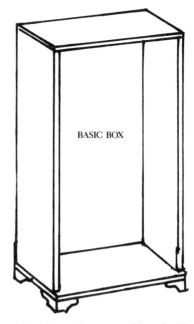

89-8.   *Assembled box. (Courtesy of Stanley Tools.)*

8d nails and wood glue, four nails to a butt joint, assemble the sides, top, and bottom. The bottom will extend ¾″ to the front of the sides and top. Make sure the assembly is square.

With the box on sawhorses, front facing down, add the back of ¼″ A-C plywood. Make sure the A side faces inside the armoire box. If you need to plane the back to get an exact fit, do so. Fasten with glue and box nails at 8″ intervals. Work in one direction as you go, and square each corner as you come to it.

For the legs, cut four 3″ × two-by-two stock, and attach T-nuts to the bottom of the armoire, in the ⅜″ holes. Drill ¼″ holes in each leg center, and attach leg to base with ⁵⁄₁₆″ hanger bolt and T-nut. Use 4d finishing nails to attach trim. Nail the cushion glides on to provide floor protection.

The armoire interior will vary depending on intended use. For the wardrobe version, do *not* cut the center divider into an L shape, as you do for the computer version. The center divider should be a full 72″ tall and 22″ deep, with no cuts. The divider may also be omitted and a full-width closet bar added. Consider a half closet bar and a series of shelves on the other half, set onto cleats, or set into shelf standards with supports. Either is easy to do.

Exterior features depend on what you would prefer, too. Doors are ripped to width at 21³⁄₁₆″ each. You may need to crosscut them, at 68½″. Make sure the cuts are square. Then, apply door trim, according to your preference. Use moulding with glue and 16-gauge 1″ brads. Lay the doors flush against the outer edges, top and

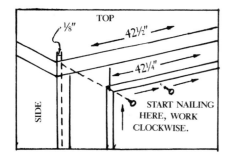

89-9. *Back nailing. (Courtesy of Stanley Tools.)*

bottom lip, with a ⅛″ center clearance for later adding of edging and needed door clearance for opening.

Leave ¹⁄₁₆″ top clearance, and measure down 3″ from the top of each door, and up 3″ from the bottom. Mark the hinge locations, and center the third hinge.

Once the marks are all made, you may attach any inside door pieces. Lay the doors, with hinges mounted, back on the box and check the marks. Use the dovetail saw to cut ¹⁄₁₆″ down on each hinge mark. Chisel out that space. Screw in the hinges, and attach the doors.

Trim the base edge with ¾″ moulding. Mitre corners, and glue and nail with 1″ brads. Use the 2¾″ crown moulding for top trim. The type of crown moulding suggested needs compound mitre cuts. Start with the *bottom* of the moulding in the mitre box, facing *up*. Measurement is from the bottom edge because that's the edge that attaches to the box. Make a 45-degree cut, check the measurement, and reverse the saw blade. Slide the crown moulding across to the length mark, and make the second cut. Side pieces butt flush at the back, so need only a single 45-degree cut each. The crown moulding goes on 2¼″ down from the top edge, with brads and glue used. Countersink and fill all holes.

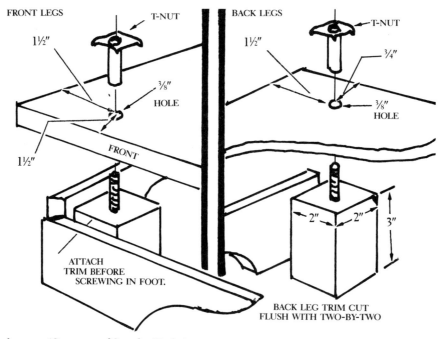

89-10. *Leg attachment. (Courtesy of Stanley Tools.)*

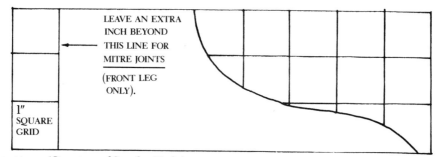

89-11. *Trim pattern. (Courtesy of Stanley Tools.)*

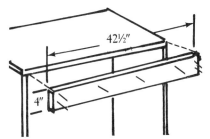

89-12. *Valance also adds rigidity. (Courtesy of Stanley Tools.)*

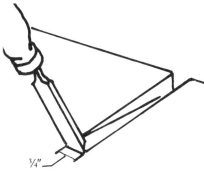

89-13. *Chiseling divider. (Courtesy of Stanley Tools.)*

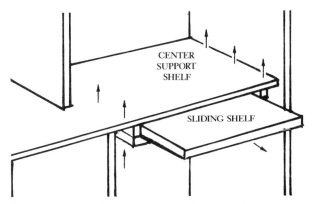

89-15. *Sliding shelf assembled. (Courtesy of Stanley Tools.)*

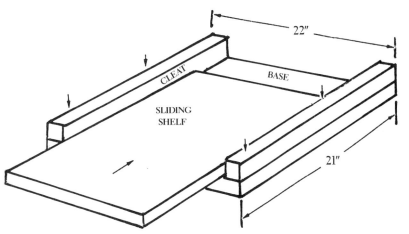

89-16. *Sliding shelf. (Courtesy of Stanley Tools.)*

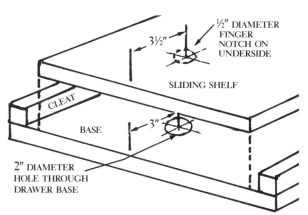

89-14. *Sliding shelf detail. (Courtesy of Stanley Tools.)*

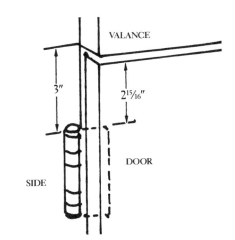

89-17. *Hinge location. (Courtesy of Stanley Tools.)*

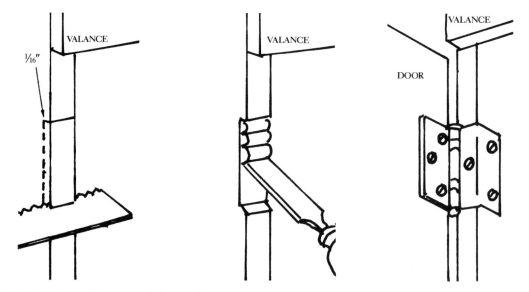

89 18.   *Installing hinge. (Courtesy of Stanley Tools.)*

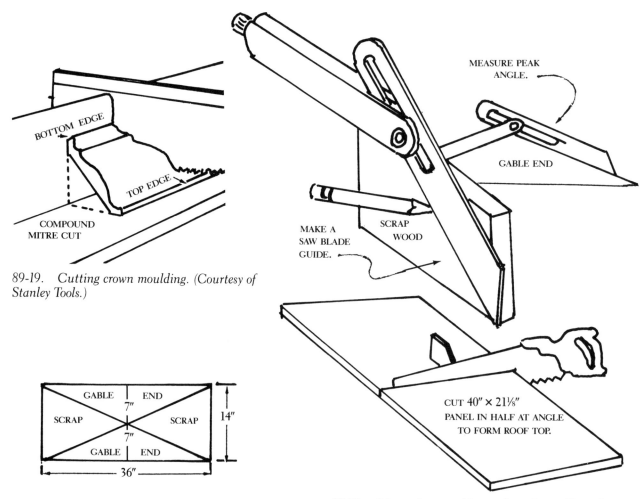

89-19.   *Cutting crown moulding. (Courtesy of Stanley Tools.)*

89-20.   *Gable end pattern. (Courtesy of Stanley Tools.)*

89-21.   *Measuring, marking and cutting gable end. (Courtesy of Stanley Tools.)*

Roof gables may be added, but are optional. There is plenty of scrap ¾″ material to form these parts if you want. Cover exposed plywood edges with iron-on wood, and add the magnetic catches for the doors. Sand, finish, and add the doorknobs.

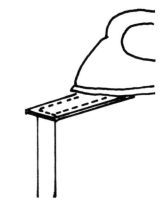

89-22. *Gable end assembly, and covering plywood edges. (Courtesy of Stanley Tools.)*

90 ◆ Computer Stand Armoire

If, like many people today, you are having trouble finding a sensible hideaway for your office at home, the armoire may provide a great solution, with space enough for even large computers and many accessories.

Materials and Tools (**Same as for Project 89**)

Follow the instructions for the armoire (Project 89) to assemble the basic box. Attach the legs and cushion glides, but cut the center divider as described here. For the computer stand, cut the center divider to an L shape,

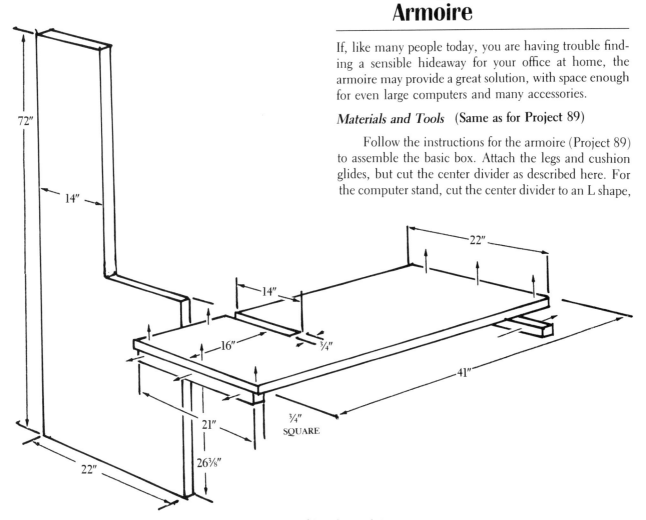

90-1. *Shelf layout, for computer armoire. (Courtesy of Stanley Tools.)*

after cutting it to its 72" × 22" size. The cut is made, from the front, 26⅜" up from the bottom, and 8" in from the front, leaving a 14" wide back panel. The middle shelf is then 22" deep, set on two 21" × ¾" × 1" cleats. Cut a slot ¾" wide, 14" deep, and 16" from the left inside to the left edge. This will fit onto the L-shaped divider, with the front leg of the divider becoming a support for the shelf. Drill and install cleats with No. 8 × 1¼" screws.

Cut the sliding shelf 1⅝" narrower than the base to allow for cleats on both sides of the drawer, plus some space for easy sliding. Cut and attach cleats to the drawer base with No. 8 × 1¼" screws, three per cleat. Use a hole saw to drill a 2" hole, 3" on center through the drawer base. The underside of the sliding shelf works best with a finger notch, about ½" in diameter, and ½" deep. Attach the completed sliding drawer assembly to the underside of the center support shelf with No. 8 × 2" screws.

Install shelf standards where desired, and use shelf clips to place shelves as needed. Shelves should be cut as needed from scrap stock.

Exterior doors are ripped to width at 21³⁄₁₆" each.

Crosscut them at 68½". Make sure cuts are square. Apply door trim, according to how you want to have it. Use moulding with glue and 16-gauge 1" brads. Lay the doors flush against the outer edges, top and bottom lip, with a ⅛" center clearance for adding edging later and for needed door clearance for opening.

Leave ¹⁄₁₆" top clearance, and measure down 3" from the top of each door, and up 3" from the bottom. Mark the hinge locations, and center the third hinge. Once the marks are all made, you may attach any inside door pieces. Lay the doors, with hinges mounted, back on the box and check the marks. Use the dovetail saw to cut ¹⁄₁₆" down on each hinge mark. Chisel out. Screw in the hinges, and attach the doors.

Trim the base edge with ¾" moulding. Mitre corners, and glue and nail with 1" brads. Use the 2¾" crown moulding for top trim. Cut the moulding as described in Project 89.

Roof gables are optional. There is plenty of scrap ¾" material to form these parts if you want. Cover exposed plywood edges with iron-on wood, and add the magnetic catches for the doors. Sand, finish, and add the doorknobs.

7 ◆ Projects Just for Kids

I doubt there's anyone working with wood who hasn't considered making a project just for a child, somewhere, sometime. For those who haven't, maybe it's about time to do so.

91 ◆ Stagecoach Toy Box

Here's a fun-to-build project that will bring joy to both children and their parents—a place to put at least some of the toy overload!

Start by marking the pieces out, as shown in the plan drawing, on the sheet of ½″ A-B sanded plywood. There is almost no waste in this project, so use care in laying things out; if you mess up, you'll have to buy a second sheet, or at least part of a sheet.

Cut out all of the parts. Glue and nail supports (O, P, Q) to sides (H, I). See the side view. Screw hinges to door (E), and then to side (H).

Now, start assembling with the sides, and floor, using glue and nails. Add the front and back, squaring the assembly where needed.

91-1.   *Stagecoach toy box. (Courtesy of the American Plywood Association.)*

Materials

- ½″ × 4′ × 8′ A-B interior sanded plywood
- two 1⁵⁄₁₆″-diameter dowels, 22″ long (axles)
- 1⁵⁄₁₆″-diameter dowel, 8″ long (for tongue assembly)
- twelve ½″ half-rounds, 1⅛″ long (front-wheel spokes)
- twelve ½″ half-rounds, 2⅛″ long (rear-wheel spokes)
- two 1½″ × 1½″ hinges
- 3″ utility pull (door handle)
- 6d finishing nails
- No. 6 × 1″ wood screws
- wood glue
- wood filler
- 120-grit sandpaper
- paint, as needed

Assemble (glue and nail) setback (S), seat (D), and foot rest (F) to sides and to supports (O, P, Q). Glue and nail two corner blocks (W) to the rear-wheel holders (T), and to the front-wheel holders (U). Complete assembly to floor of the coach box.

Assemble the wheels, and attach them to the axles. Glue and nail the tongue holders (N) to the floor, then screw the tongue parts (G) together at the handle end and at the tongue dowel.

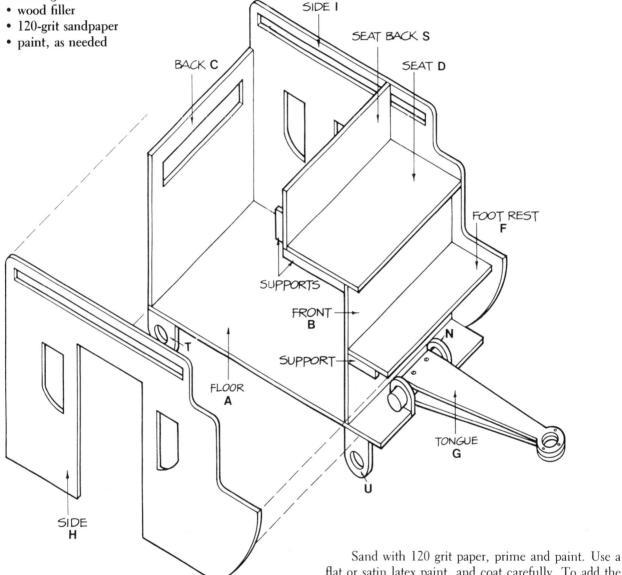

91-2. *Exploded drawing. (Courtesy of the American Plywood Association.)*

Sand with 120 grit paper, prime and paint. Use a flat or satin latex paint, and coat carefully. To add the lettering and decorative striping shown in the photograph, start at your office supply store. Press-on letters in many styles and sizes are available, as is press-on striping. To keep the lettering and striping looking good over time, coat with a clear finish.

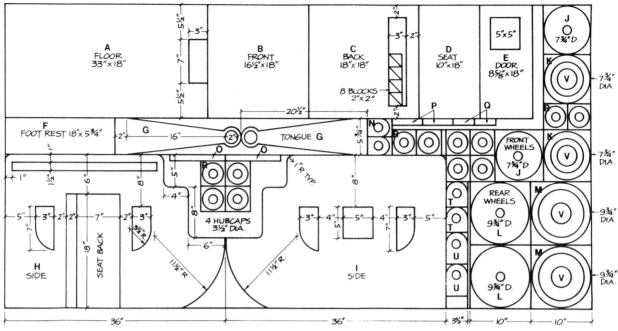

91-3. *Panel layout. (Courtesy of the American Plywood Association.)*

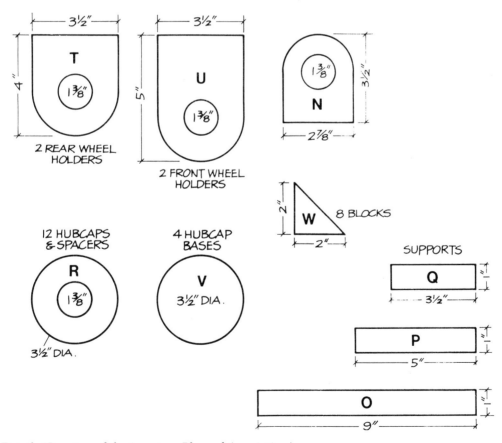

91-4. *Detail. (Courtesy of the American Plywood Association.)*

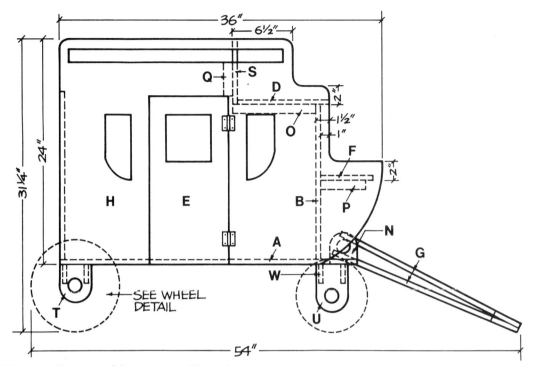

91-5. *Side view. (Courtesy of the American Plywood Association.)*

Tools
- circular saw
- saw guide
- scroll saw or jigsaw
- screwdriver
- measuring tape
- square
- large compass or trammel points and bar
- awl
- hammer
- nail set
- pad sander

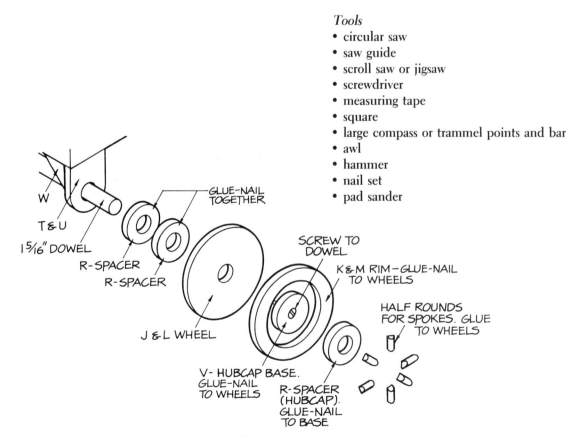

91-6. *Wheels. (Courtesy of the American Plywood Association.)*

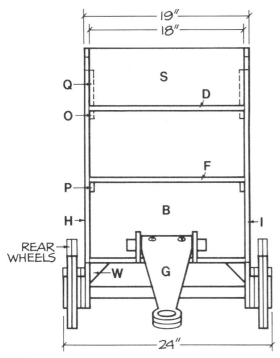

91-7. *Front view. (Courtesy of the American Plywood Association.)*

92 ♦ Junior Tool Box

Tool boxes are simple projects, whether for adults or children, and this version is even easier than most. It is a reduced-size version of a carpenter's tool box.

Materials
- one-by-ten × 48″ pine, or one-quarter sheet of ¾″ birch plywood
- ½″ × 6″ × 48″ pine
- 1″ × 24″ dowel
- 6d finishing nails
- wood glue

Tools
- saw
- scroll saw or jigsaw
- square
- measuring tape
- hammer
- nail set
- 100-grit sandpaper
- drill, ¼″, ⅜″ bit, 1″ bit, preferably a Forstner
- C-clamp

92-1. *Junior tool box. (Courtesy of Stanley Tools.)*

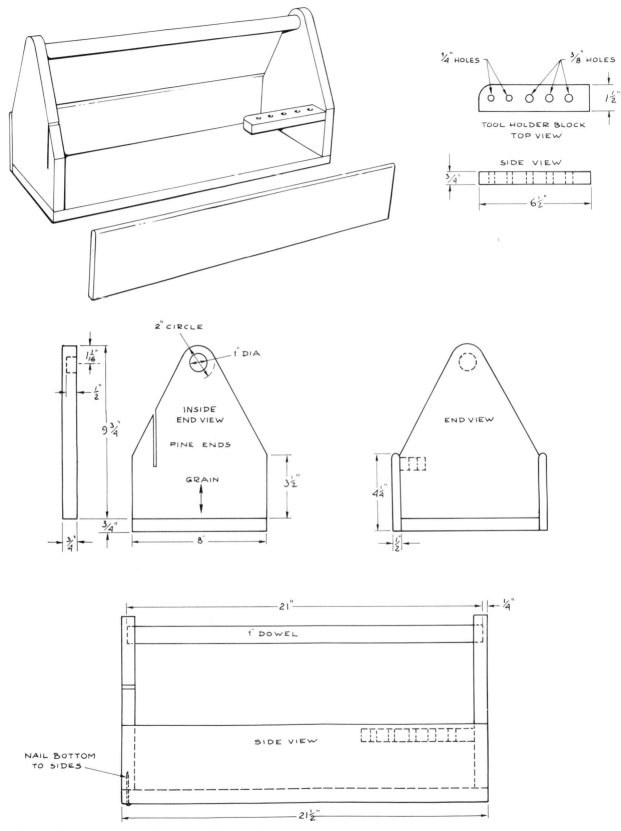

¼" HOLES

⅜" HOLES

TOOL HOLDER BLOCK
TOP VIEW

SIDE VIEW

1½"

¾"

6½"

2" CIRCLE

1" DIA

INSIDE
END VIEW

PINE ENDS

GRAIN

END VIEW

1 1/16"

½"

9¾"

¾"

¾"

3½"

8"

4¼"

½"

21"

¼"

1" DOWEL

SIDE VIEW

NAIL BOTTOM
TO SIDES

21½"

92-2.   *Tool box drawing. (Courtesy of Stanley Tools.)*

Start by cutting all of the pieces to sizes shown on plan drawing. Drill five holes (¼″ and ⅜″) in the tool holder. Cut a ³⁄₁₆″ wide slot in one end piece. Smooth all edges.

Use the Forstner bit to drill a ½″ deep hole in each end piece, centered on a 2″ circle below the top radius.

Assemble the dowel and end pieces, after which the sides are added with wood glue and 6d finishing nails. Set the nails flush with the wood surface, not below, unless you plan to use wood putty to fill the resulting holes, and then paint the tool box. Add the bottom next, then glue the tool-holder block in place. Clamp the block for a couple of hours.

Add tools and the child's eyes will light up.

I recommend the following tools for children ages 9 to 12: 13-ounce claw hammer; 26″ crosscut saw; coping saw; screwdriver set; 8′ tape measure; block plane; safety goggles; hand drill; 18″ wood level; combination square; bar clamp; workshop apron.

93 ◆ Girl's Vanity

This project gets cosmetics, lotions, and similar items up and out of the way, while also providing space for toy animals, small stereos, and other items, along with a mirror.

Materials

- 1″ × 10″ × 72″ A-A interior plywood
- four ¾″ × 11¼″ × 34½″ particle board
- ten 1″ × 12″ × 20″ A-A interior plywood
- two 1″ × 19¼″ × 34½″ A-A interior plywood
- plywood edging tape
- one-by-twelve × 72″ pine or fir
- eight 12″ shelf brackets, to fit standards
- two 48″ shelf standards
- twelve wall anchors and screws
- No. 10 × 1½″ flathead brass wood screws
- forty-four brass grommets
- No. 10 × 2″ flathead brass wood screws
- T-nuts
- 30″ × 36″ mirror
- four plastic mirror brackets
- six ¾″ diameter × 6″ dowels
- wood glue
- wood filler
- stain
- tung oil
- paint
- 120-grit sandpaper

Cut all plywood and particle board to the sizes shown, after laying out the cuts on the sheets. Sand and make sure edges are smooth, but not rounded-over.

93-1. Girl's wall vanity. (Courtesy of Georgia-Pacific Corporation.)

Tools

- circular saw
- saw guide
- drill, ¾″ brad point bit, ³⁄₃₂″, ³⁄₁₆″ drill bits
- countersink
- jointer or bench plane
- tape measure
- square
- bar clamps
- level
- screwdriver or driver bit for clutched drill
- pad sander
- paint brush

Drill pilot holes for 1½″ screws and assemble the vanity, using screws, grommets, and glue. Drill ¾″ holes, on 6″ centers, on the overhead board, along the board midline. These accept the 6″ dowels, which are now glued in place.

Check vanity height needs: the user should have the vanity bottom about 2″ above her knees when seated comfortably in a chair. Use eight 2″ wood screws to hit the studs in back of the vanity for support. For better support at legs at the front two edges, cut two-by-two pine to length, and, if desired, taper on a table saw, jointer, or with a plane. Drive a T-nut into the top center of each leg (after drilling to accept the T-nut), and drill holes through the vanity bottom to accept the matching machine screws or bolts.

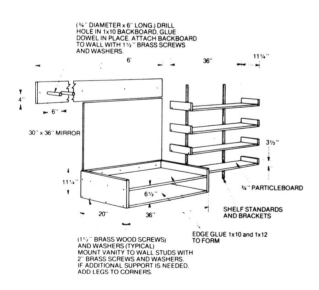

93-2. *Vanity drawing. (Courtesy of Georgia-Pacific Corporation.)*

Mount the overhead board above the mirror. Mount the mirror with the four mirror wall brackets, using hollow wall anchors as needed. The overhead board is fastened in place with 1½″ brass wood screws and grommets. Try to hit at least two wall studs.

Mount the shelf standards, either on wall studs or with hollow wall anchors. Attach sides to shelves using 1½″ brass wood screws and grommets, and glue. Install the shelf brackets and insert the shelves.

Finishing is up to you, but overall a clear finish on some better-looking wood parts contrasts nicely with a painted finish on shelving. If you wish, you may leave out the grommets and lightly countersink all screw holes.

94 ◆ Moving Van

Push toys are always popular with children. This van is designed for use by children from three to eight years of age. It is a useful size, has a removable top, and is enjoyable to look at.

Tools

- hand or circular saw
- keyhole saw
- coping saw
- square
- measuring tape
- pad sander
- screwdriver
- adjustable wrench, 8″
- wood rasp
- wood chisel, ¾″
- drill, ³⁄₁₆″, ¼″, ½″ bits
- bar clamps

Start by cutting all of the pieces to size, cutting the two-by-four into 5″ pieces, three of which are glued and clamped together to make the hood. For the cab sides, drill a starter hole, and use the keyhole saw to cut the basic window shape. Cut the fender outlines with a coping saw. Smooth all cab and fender contours with a wood rasp or other tool.

The underside of the chassis is carved with the wood chisel, forming four concave wheel wells ¾″ wide. Drill four ³⁄₁₆″ pilot holes 1¾″ deep in the ends of two axle blocks so they hold the axle bolts. Drill two holes ¼″ diameter by ½″ deep in the opposite edges of the van end and to matching holes in the van sides for the dowel pivots. Glue dowels in place in the van end.

Drill a hole ½″ in diameter by ⅜″ deep on the outside of the van door bottom for the dowel handle. Glue the dowel in place.

Materials
- one-by-eight × 96″ pine, or fir
- two-by-four × 24″ pine, or fir
- 1⅛″ × 1¾″ × 7″ pine, or fir
- ¼″, ½″, ¾″ dowel stock (3′ lengths)
- eight No. 6 × 1¼″ flathead wood screws
- four ¼″ × 3″ hex-head lag screws
- eight ½″ diameter washers, with ¼″ holes
- wood glue
- 120-grit sandpaper
- polyurethane

Use wood glue to assemble and clamp the following parts (do dry-assemblies first to assure a correct fit): the chassis to the two axle blocks; hood to two cab sides to roof; van bottom to the two van sides to van end. Countersink four holes for No. 6 wood screws in the van bottom and install the screws up into the van sides.

When the above steps have rested long enough for glue to dry thoroughly (at least two hours), glue the cab assembly and van assembly to the chassis assembly. Countersink four holes for No. 6 wood screws in chassis and run screws into the van bottom.

94-1.   *Moving van. (Courtesy of Stanley Tools.)*

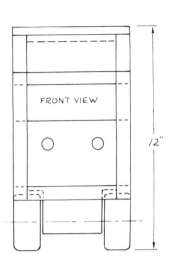

FRONT VIEW

12"

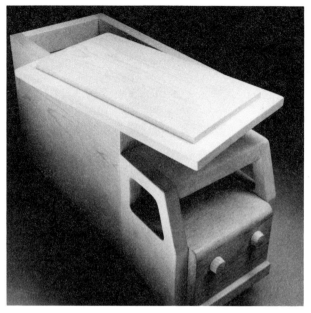

94-3. Assembly. (Courtesy of Stanley Tools.)

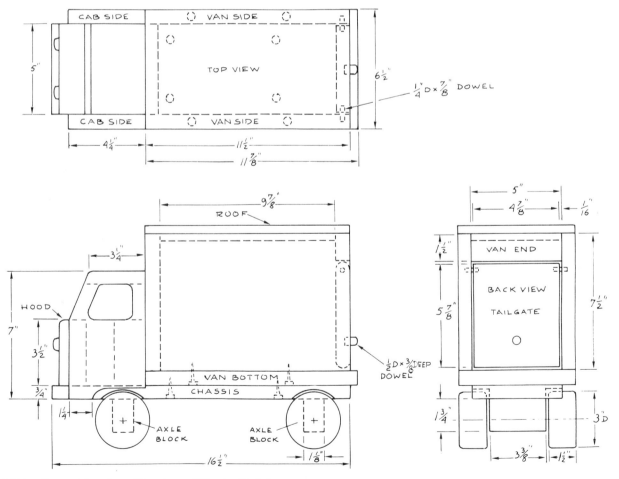

CAB SIDE   VAN SIDE

TOP VIEW

CAB SIDE   VAN SIDE

5"

6½"

$\frac{1}{4}$" D × $\frac{7}{8}$" DOWEL

4¼"

11½"

11⅞"

9⅞"

ROOF

3¼"

HOOD

7"

3½"

¾"

VAN BOTTOM

CHASSIS

AXLE BLOCK

AXLE BLOCK

¼"

16½"

1⅛"

$\frac{1}{2}$" D × $\frac{3}{8}$" DEEP DOWEL

5"

4⅞"

$\frac{1}{16}$"

1½"

VAN END

BACK VIEW

TAILGATE

5⅞"

7½"

1¾"

3 D

3⅜"

1½"

94-2. Layout drawing. (Courtesy of Stanley Tools.)

The strongest top is made, and left removable, by gluing a 5″ × 9⅞″ second board under the actual top, centered in both directions.

Make wheels of hardwood, if possible, or of a hard softwood such as Southern pine. Use ¾″ dimension stock, and cut the 3″ diameter wheels with the coping saw (or a scroll or band saw, or, in fact, a 3″ hole saw). Smooth edges with sandpaper. Assemble the wheels and axles (the ¼″ × 3″ lag bolts and washers for both sides of each wheel). Glue two wheel sections per wheel, aiming to get grain directions at right angles. No glue is needed when the axles are screwed into the axle holes.

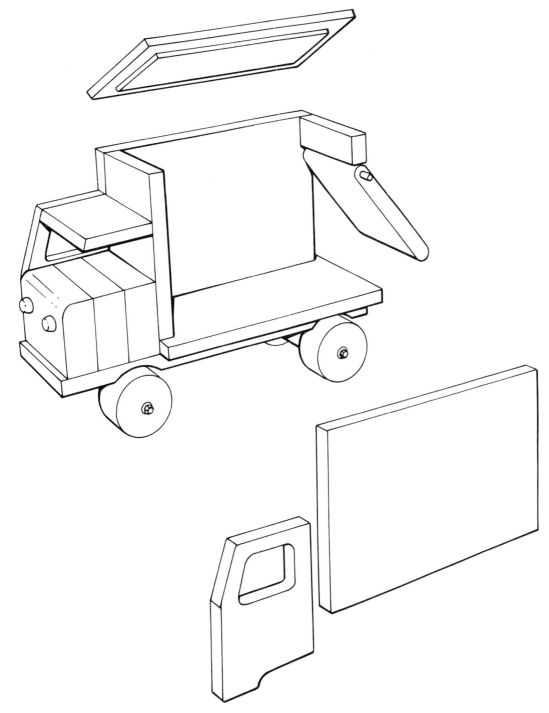

94-4. *Exploded drawing. (Courtesy of Stanley Tools.)*

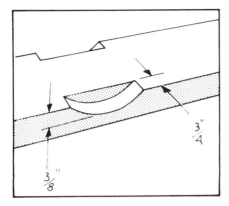

94-5. *Wheel well drawings. (Courtesy of Stanley Tools.)*

To make headlights, cut two ¾″ lengths of ¾″ diameter dowel, shape the edges with sandpaper, and then glue them in place on the hood.

With solid wood used throughout, this van will look best with either no stain, or a light-colored stain, and a spray-on polyurethane finish that will take the battering that constant use will give this toy.

94-6. *Assembled wheel. (Courtesy of Stanley Tools.)*

95 ♦ Marble Chase

This project is designed for children old enough to play with marbles, which generally means four years and up. If the child cannot handle marbles, store the project for the following Christmas or birthday.

Materials
- one-by-one × 48″ pine baluster
- ¾″ × 4″ × 48″ pine
- one-quarter sheet ¼″ fir or hardwood plywood (A-A if fir)
- ⅜″ × 12″ dowel
- No. 8 × 1½″ flathead wood screws
- wood glue
- masking tape
- paint
- 120-grit sandpaper

Tools
- circular saw
- coping saw, or scroll saw, or jigsaw
- mitre box and backsaw
- screwdriver
- measuring tape
- square
- protractor
- sliding T bevel
- drill, ⅜″ and ½″ brad point bits, 11/16″ drill bit
- countersink
- 6 C-clamps
- surform
- pad sander

Start by cutting the plywood pieces, using masking tape over the cut lines to reduce splintering. Then, cut the remainder of the pieces, from the drawings, making sure you finish with 10 four-by-four blocks. Four are designed in, with the remaining six used to change slopes. Use the mitre box and backsaw to cut angles on parts where angles are needed: transfer angles from the plan to the parts with a protractor and sliding T bevel.

You may want to cut parts for C2 and D separately with a coping or scroll saw. It's just as easy to cut part D's six pieces to basic shape with the mitre box, and then to shape, after clamping them together, to final form.

Bevel the catch basin base to give an even slope from a ¾″ thickness at one end to half that (⅜″) at the other end. Drill three ½″ holes through each track base, and then drill a blind dowel hole in the catch basin and the top end of each support pole. Countersink and add a pilot hole in each support hole bottom for the wood screw.

Glue dowels into four support poles and the catch basin. Glue the catch basin lip to the base. Glue up the track sections: glue one end of the section to the base, then to the two long side pieces, then to the other end piece. To position the small interior pieces, run masking tape down the length of each side piece. Mark the positions of the interior pieces on the tape, and you can just peel off pencil marks instead of later having to sand them off.

Use tape to "clamp" small pieces while glue dries. Tape may also be used to set the pieces temporarily so you can check the roll of marbles and make any changes.

If painting is to be done in contrasting colors, paint the top and sides of the pieces before gluing them up. This saves a lot of fancy fine work with a brush.

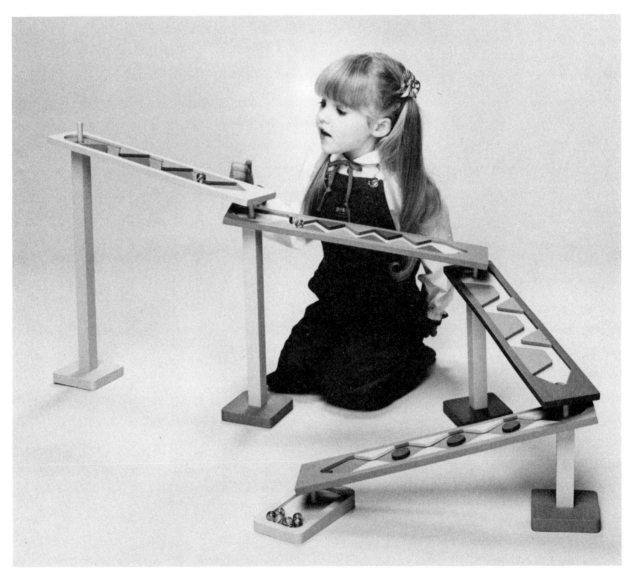

95-1.   *Marble chase. (Courtesy of Stanley Tools.)*

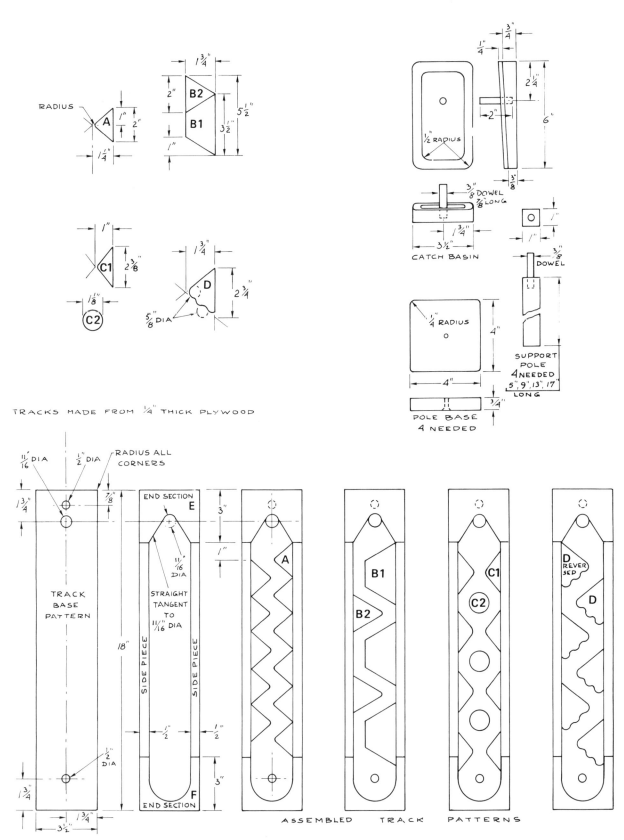

TRACKS MADE FROM ¼" THICK PLYWOOD

CATCH BASIN

POLE BASE
4 NEEDED

SUPPORT
POLE
4 NEEDED
5", 9", 13", 17"
LONG

TRACK
BASE
PATTERN

ASSEMBLED   TRACK   PATTERNS

95-2.   *Layout drawing. (Courtesy of Stanley Tools.)*

136

95-3. *Catch basin. (Courtesy of Stanley Tools.)*

Marbles jumping the track means you need to check the high end of the support post in any problem section. Make sure the post is square with the track so there's no wobble. If the decline is too steep, use the extra four-by-four blocks to prop up the low post.

96 ◆ Ferry Boat

This "working" boat may be filled with toy cars, the design specifically scaled to hold toy cars 4½" to 5" long. Smaller ones will also work, but may look a little dwarfed.

Materials
- ½" × 13¼" × 22¾" hardwood plywood, plywood, or wood core (car deck)
- ½" × 11¾" × 16⅜" hardwood plywood, plywood, or wood core (top deck)
- two ¾" × 4½" × 14⅜" walnut, cherry, etc. (cabin side walls)
- two ¾" × 3¼" × 7" walnut, cherry, etc. (cabin front and rear walls)
- ½" × 6¾" × 8" hardwood plywood (cabin roof)
- ½" × 5½" diameter hardwood plywood (cabin top roof)
- two ½" × ½" × 5¾" hardwood plywood (cabin roof-securing strips)
- 1" × 3" dowel (smokestack)
- two ½" × 1" × 14¾" walnut, cherry, etc. (top deck side rails)
- six ⅜" × 1⅜" dowels (rope rail posts)
- two ½" × 1¼" × 11" walnut, cherry (car deck gates)

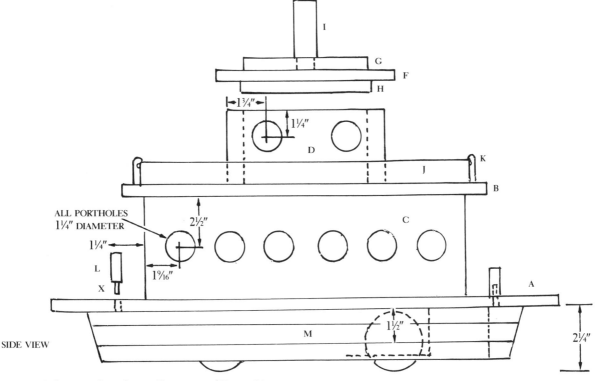

96-1. *Side view, ferry boat. (Courtesy of Dremel.)*

- one hull (series of plywood rings, see text)
- two ¾″ × 2″ × 11″ pine (wheel supports)
- two ⅜″ × 7½″ dowels (axles)
- four 2½″ diameter wheels
- two ⅜″ × ⅜″ × 11″ walnut, cherry (car dividers)
- six 2″ dry-wall screws (hull to deck)
- four 1¾″ drive screws (axle supports to deck)
- twelve 1½″ drive screws (side walls to top/car deck)
- four 1½″ drive screws (cabin to top deck)
- eight 1⅜″ × ⅛″ pins (side rails to top deck)
- twenty 1″ × ⅛″ pins (corners of cabin)
- four 1″ × ⅜″ dowels (gate to car deck)
- sixteen ¾″ brass escutcheon pins
- braided twine, for rail rope, as needed
- 120-grit sandpaper
- clear finish

Tools
- table or handsaw
- scroll saw
- power sander
- router, ¼″ round-over bit
- drill, ⅛″ bit, ⅜″ and 1″ brad point bits, 1¼″ Forstner bit
- ⅜″ dowel points
- pad sander
- six small bar clamps

A CAR DECK
B TOP DECK
C CAR DECK WALLS
D CABIN SIDE WALLS
E CABIN FRONT/REAR WALLS
F CABIN ROOF
G CABIN TOP ROOF
H CABIN ROOF-SECURING STRIPS
I STACK
J TOP DECK SIDE RAILS
K ROPE RAIL POSTS
L CAR DECK GATES
M HULL
N WHEEL SUPPORTS
O AXLES
P WHEELS
Q CAR DIVIDERS
S SCREW AXLE SUPPORTS TO DECK.
T SCREW SIDE WALLS TO TOP/CAR DECK.
R SCREW HULL TO DECK.
U SCREW CABIN TO TOP DECK.
V PIN SIDE RAILS TO TOP DECK.
W PIN CORNERS OF CABIN.
X DOWELS FOR GATE TO CAR DECK
Y BRASS ESCUTCHEON PINS
Z RAIL ROPE

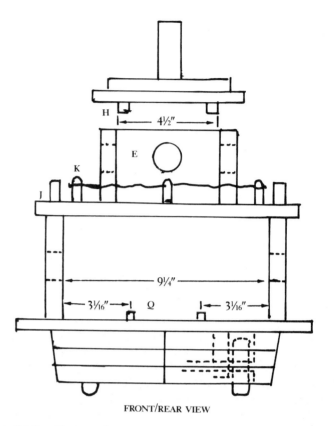

FRONT/REAR VIEW

96-2. *Front and rear view. (Courtesy of Dremel.)*

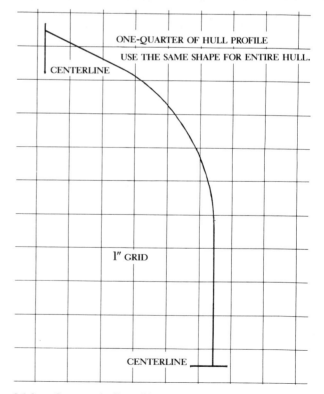

ONE-QUARTER OF HULL PROFILE

USE THE SAME SHAPE FOR ENTIRE HULL.

CENTERLINE

1″ GRID

CENTERLINE

96-3. *Quarter hull profile. (Courtesy of Dremel.)*

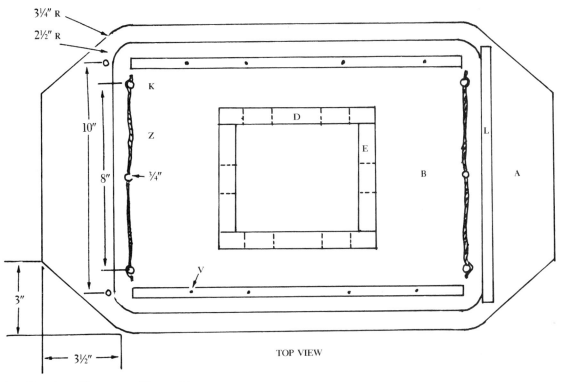

3¼" R

2½" R

10"

8"

3"

3½"

K

Z

¾"

V

D

E

B

L

A

TOP VIEW

96-4. *Top view. (Courtesy of Dremel.)*

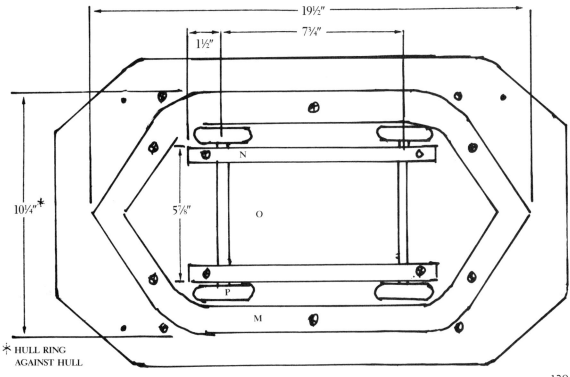

19½"

7¾"

1½"

10¼" ✳

5⅞"

N

O

P

M

✳ HULL RING
AGAINST HULL

96-5. *Bottom view. (Courtesy of Dremel.)*   BOTTOM VIEW

Hull height needs to be about 2″, which means you must cut enough plywood rings to allow that height. Rings are bevelled, and reduced in size as they go *down* to the floor. Use an outline for the top ring from the drawing, getting it 19½″ long at the points. Bevel at 10 degrees on the outside, and use the inside to get the next ring size. For a pleasing hull shape, use ½″ plywood for four pieces, or two pieces of ¾″ and one of ½″.

Glue the pieces together, and clamp them together or to a flat surface (preferable). Let dry and shape on the sander for final shape.

Paint the hull now, if you wish. Do not coat the top surface that will go against the deck bottom.

Cut and round all corners on the two decks, and cut the remaining pieces. Drill portholes in the cabin top pieces, and car deck walls. Drill rope railing holes to a depth of ⅜″. Drill gate holes all the way through the main deck.

Assemble and glue up the cabin. Clamp until the glue dries. Then drill ⅛″ holes through both pieces at the corners and drive dowels into those holes. Sand or saw off excess dowel. When the glue has dried, remove clamps and rout a round-over on all cabin edges. Sand. Drill pilot holes from underneath the top deck and attach the cabin to the top deck with screws and glue.

The car divider strips are secured with brass pins and glue on the car deck. Glue and screw on the axle supports and wheel assemblies on the underside of the car deck. Make sure screws don't come up through the deck, and make sure the axles and wheels don't rub.

Now, assemble the top deck, car deck, and car deck walls with glue and screws. Drill pilot holes through decks and into walls and countersink all screw heads.

Attach the top and side rails with glue and ⅛″ wood dowel pins. Cut away any excess dowel (or sand). Attach the hull to the car deck. Drill pilot holes through the hull, making them a bit larger than the screw diameter.

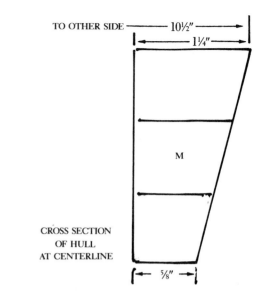

96-7. *Hull cross section. (Courtesy of Dremel.)*

Make sure screws will *not* penetrate car deck. The oversize pilot holes in the *hull* let the screws draw the pieces tightly together.

Drill ⅛″ holes through railing posts and round-over the tops. Do any finishing work intended on these before gluing them in their holes. Wrap tape around the part that will receive glue before finishing.

Figure the locations for the gate-securing pins. Drill ⅜″ diameter holes into the gate, and glue dowels in place. Trim the dowels so they project ½″. Drill holes in the car deck to mate with dowel projections.

Shape the cabin roof with a sander and round over all available edges with a router. The roof is held in place with two strips of wood, which are glued and pinned to the underside of the roof to fit inside the cabin. Allow ¹⁄₁₆″ between cabin walls and the strips. Center the circular roof on top, and fasten with glue and brass pins. Drill a 1″ × ½″ deep hole in the cabin roof to accept the dowel smokestack. Glue the stack in place.

Check the project for splinters, and rough spots, and scrape off any dried glue. Sand, and finish.

97 ◆ Easel Bench

This easy and economical project—just half a sheet of ⅜″plywood is the main materials need—provides hours of fun with its varied features. The easel bench has an adjustable chalkboard, movable bench, book bin, and side shelf.

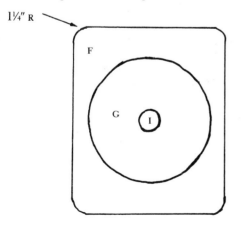

96-6. *Top. (Courtesy of Dremel.)*

Materials

- 48″ × 48″ × ⅜″ medium-density overlay or A-B sanded plywood
- ½″ × 24″ dowel
- ½″ × 2″ dowel
- 1½″ wood knob
- thirty No. 6 1½″ drive screws
- one pint blackboard paint
- ¼″ × ¾″ × 24″ screen moulding
- 2d and 4d finishing nails
- wood filler
- wood glue
- 120-grit sandpaper

Draw the parts layout on the back of the plywood sheet, and cut out the parts. Assemble the struts and storage box sides, nailing and gluing cleats, as shown. Nail and glue the desk sides to the storage box and struts.

Assemble the tabletop, shelf, and seat, and sand carefully. Paint with your choice of colors, using a good-quality latex paint. For the blackboard tabletop, apply blackboard paint following manufacturer's directions.

When paint is dry, position the tabletop, seat, and shelf, as shown. Use the 24″ dowel to hold the table in place at the desired angle. Insert the 2″ dowel in the wood knob, and insert in the second easel position to add stability.

97-1. *Easel bench. (Courtesy of the American Plywood Association.)*

Tools

- handsaw or circular saw
- measuring tape
- square
- drill, ⅛″ and 3/16″ bits, ½″ brad point bit
- hammer
- nail set
- alphabet stencils
- paint brushes, 2″ and 3″
- stencil brush

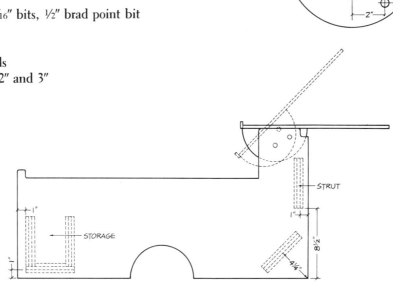

97-2. *Side view, and hinges. (Courtesy of the American Plywood Association.)*

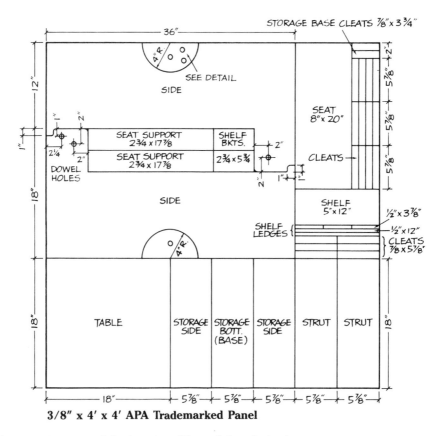

97-3. *Panel layout. (Courtesy of the American Plywood Association.)*

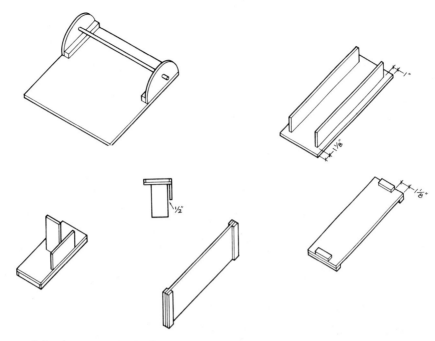

97-4. *Detail. (Courtesy of the American Plywood Association.)*

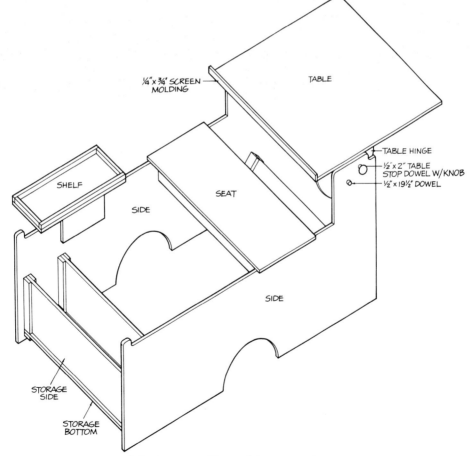

97-5. *Exploded drawing. (Courtesy of the American Plywood Association.)*

98 ♦ Wiggly Gator

Action toys are always popular with children. This wooden alligator, for children three to five, is a pull toy with an animated body. The bell on the tail is optional but does add sound effects.

Materials
- one-by-eight × 10' No. 2 pine
- 1" × 7" dowel
- twenty-two ¾" round-head machine screws and nuts
- two 2½" flathead machine screws and nuts
- 1¾" flathead machine screw and nuts
- four 1¼" plate-type casters and screws
- 4" × 1³⁄₁₆" strap hinge and screws
- 7" × 27" heavy natural-color sailcloth
- 4' heavy line
- wood glue
- white glue
- 120-grit sandpaper
- paint

Cut all of the pieces as shown on the plans, making two of each body, head, foot, and tail piece from the ¾" stock. Bevel at 45 degrees, as shown. You now need a jig, make from a board at least 4½' long by 8" wide. Attach a 4½' long piece of straight board to one edge (nail), and lay all the body parts in sequence, their side edges touching, and bottom edges lined up on the jig upright.

Tools
- handsaw
- circular saw
- scissors
- ¾" or 1" wood chisel
- hammer
- screwdriver
- angle screwdriver
- adjustable wrench
- paint brush
- pad sander
- twelve C- or short bar clamps
- drill, ³⁄₁₆", ⅝", ¹⁄₁₆", ⅛" bits, ¾" and 1½" Forstner bits

Cut the canvas that serves as the flexible web joining the pieces. The material must extend 2½" into the lower jaw on one end and 2½" into the tail piece on the other end. Trim so that it lies about ³⁄₁₆" inside the edges of the top and bottom outlines of the alligator body.

Spread white glue on the exposed side of the body, and lay the trimmed canvas over the glue. Follow the outline carefully. Cover the canvas with waxed paper, add a large board, and then clamp each section. When that dries, remove the clamps and board, and place glue on the exposed canvas. Place the remaining body parts, aligned with their matching parts, and clamp again. Let dry thoroughly.

Drill twenty-two ¹⁄₁₆" diameter pilot holes for bolts at points shown. Centered on these holes, drill ⅝" diameter holes, ⁷⁄₁₆" deep on each side. Then drill ³⁄₁₆"

98-1. *Wiggly gator. (Courtesy of Stanley Tools.)*

diameter holes completely through, following the pilot holes. Install the twenty-two ¾″ machine screws and nuts. The ⅝″ diameter holes allow use of a socket wrench to tighten the nuts. The ⅝″ holes may now be plugged, if desired.

Glue the two upper jaw pieces together. After the glue dries, drill the large holes (1½″) for the eyes and nostrils (¾″). Drill from both sides to prevent splintering (you may also clamp on a backer board so that the drill-through cannot create splinters).

Attaching the movable jaw takes some planning, and some care. Mark the six screw holes for the strap hinge in the upper and lower jaws. Attach the hinge to the upper jaw with the three furnished flathead wood screws. Drill three ³⁄₁₆″ diameter holes through the lower jaw, *perpendicular to the jaw's diagonal upper surface*, *not* to its bottom. Counterbore with ⅝″ diameter holes on the *bottom* surface of the lower jaw. Install three flathead machine screws through the lower jaw holes and the lower hinge strap holes. Use the shorter screw near the front. Add nuts, and use an angle screwdriver to tighten.

Glue and clamp the foot pieces together to make two 1½″ wide parts. Make the double dado joints as shown in the plans, using a handsaw and a ¾″ or 1″ wood chisel. Drill pilot holes, as shown, and install the casters. Glue the feet in place on the body.

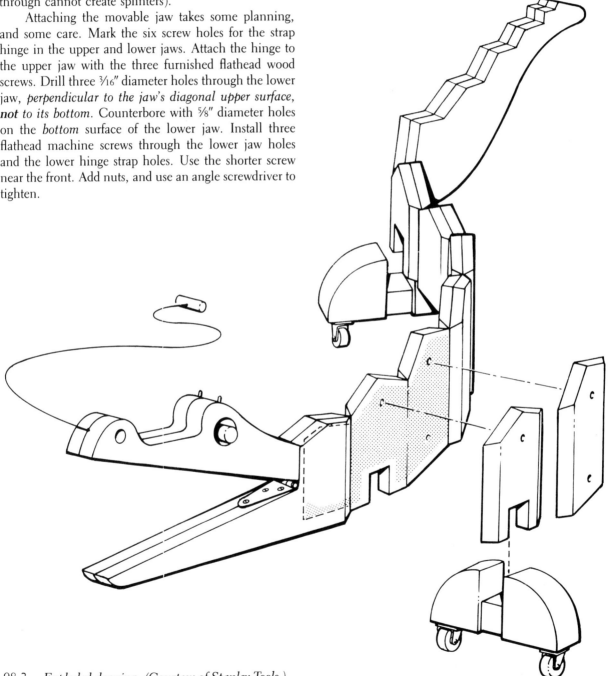

98-2.   *Exploded drawing. (Courtesy of Stanley Tools.)*

Drill two ⅛″ vertical holes into the eye cavity from above and drill two matching blind holes in the eye cylinder (the 1″ × 2¼″ dowel) to accept the cords. Glue one end of each cord in a blind hole. Thread the other end through an upper hole, and knot.

Drill the upper jaw diagonally for the pull cord. Insert the cord and knot the lower end. At the free end, attach the handle, the 1″ × 4″ center-drilled dowel. Finish to taste, using a good latex paint, and hang a toy bell on the tail tip.

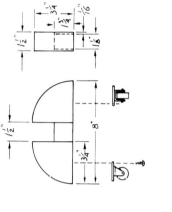

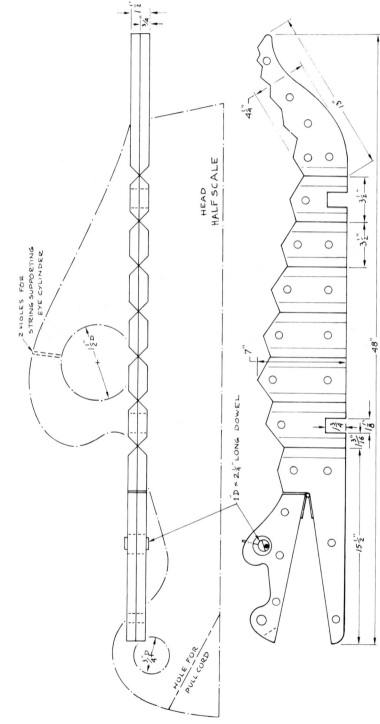

98-3. *Plan drawing. (Courtesy of Stanley Tools.)*

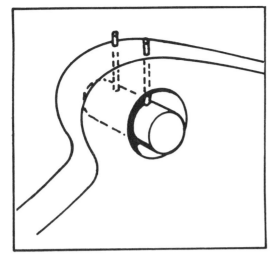

98-4. *Detail. (Courtesy of Stanley Tools.)*

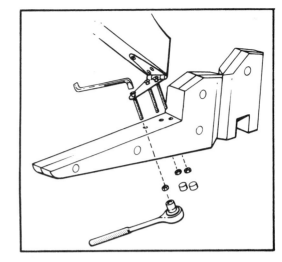

98-5. *Detail. (Courtesy of Stanley Tools.)*

98-6. *Using jig to assemble body. (Courtesy of Stanley Tools.)*

99 ♦ Teddy Bear Lamp

This lamp project is easy to do, adds a small music box "button," and pleases children.

Materials
- two-by-ten × 18″ poplar
- ⅜″ × 1½″ dowel
- lamp parts, with bent standard
- wood glue
- 120-grit sandpaper
- paint

Tools
- band saw, scroll saw, or jigsaw
- router, ½″ straight bit
- drill or drill press, ⅜″, ½″ brad point bits, ⅞″ and 1″ Forstner bits
- finishing sander
- paint brush

Start by cutting the 9″ diameter circle for the base. Drill that with the 1″ Forstner bit, 1″ deep, to take the nut off the lamp standard. Drill the center of that with the ½″ bit to accept the lamp standard. Use a router and ½″ straight bit to cut a slot for the cord.

99-1. *Teddy bear lamp.*

Cut the teddy bear to the pattern. Drill a ⅞″ hole, 1″ deep, in the back of the teddy bear. This accepts the music button. Drill a ⅜″ × ¾″ hole in the bottom of the teddy bear, and a matching hole in the base. Paint the base and the teddy bear as desired; I used pink for the base and tan for the bear. I used eyes from a general merchandise supplier with a crafts section.

Insert and glue a dowel in the base. Insert and glue the dowel in the teddy bear. Insert the lamp standard and assemble. Select a shade, and add a 25 or 40 watt bulb and you have a fine lamp for a child.

99-4. *Hole drilled for music movement.*

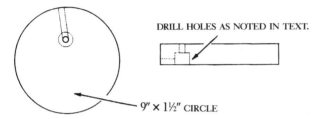

DRILL HOLES AS NOTED IN TEXT.

9″ × 1½″ CIRCLE

99-2. *Lamp base drawing.*

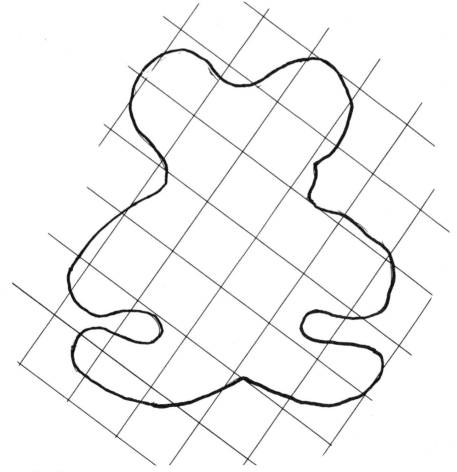

99-3. *Pattern on 1″ grid.*

149

100 ◆ Duck Lamp

This lamp is quite similar to the Teddy Bear Lamp (Project 99) above. The decorative shape is a duck, not a bear, and it is off-center instead of on.

Materials and Tools   (**Same as for Project 99**)

Cut and prepare the base following the instructions for Project 99. Then, cut the duck to the pattern.

Drill a ⅞″ hole, 1″ deep, in the back of the duck to accept the music button. Drill a ⅜″ × ¾″ deep hole in the bottom of the duck, and a matching hole in the base. Paint the base and the duck as desired; I used pink for the base and teal for the bird. I used orange eyes from the crafts section of a local store.

Insert and glue a dowel in base. Insert and glue the dowel in the duck. Insert the lamp standard and assemble. Select a shade, and add a 25 or 40 watt bulb.

100-1. Duck lamp.

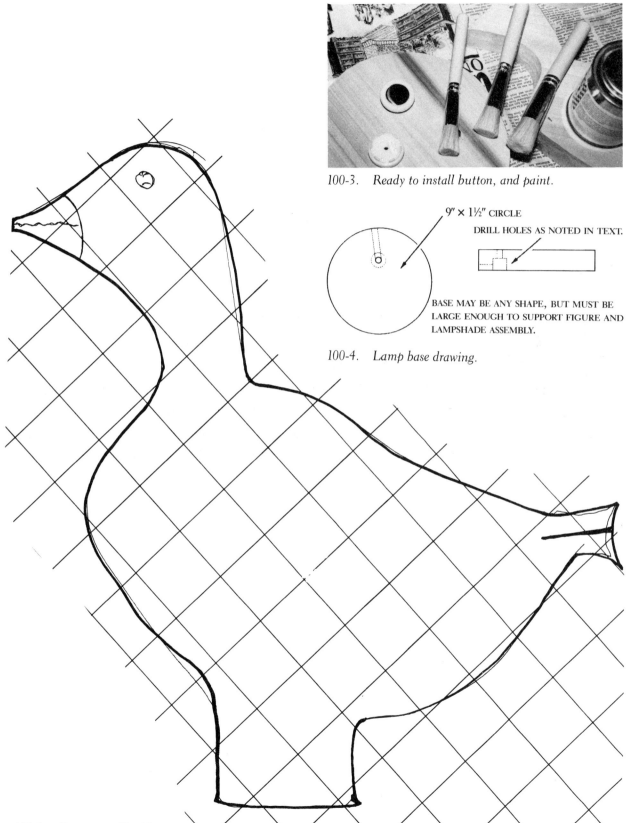

100-3. *Ready to install button, and paint.*

9″ × 1½″ CIRCLE

DRILL HOLES AS NOTED IN TEXT.

BASE MAY BE ANY SHAPE, BUT MUST BE
LARGE ENOUGH TO SUPPORT FIGURE AND
LAMPSHADE ASSEMBLY.

100-4. *Lamp base drawing.*

100-2. *Pattern on 1″ grid.*

101 ◆ Porky Bank

This bank was inspired by some music-making bank slots that I found at one of the many hardware supply houses that I use.

Materials
- three one-by-twelve × 10″ pine or other wood
- two-by-twelve × 10″ poplar or other wood
- wood glue
- paint
- 100 grit sandpaper
- musical bank slot
- rubber plug

Tools
- band saw, scroll saw, or jigsaw
- drill, ½″, 1″, 1⅛″ bits
- four 6″ bar clamps
- finishing sander
- belt sander

Start by taping blanks together, drawing on the pig pattern, and cutting with a band saw. If a band saw isn't available, cut one or two pieces at a time with a jigsaw or scroll saw.

Mark the middle three pieces with an oval that gives 1″ of clearance in the pig's back and about ¾″ in his belly. Drill two 1″ holes, and cut out with the jigsaw. Glue solid sides to the hollow center.

Drill ½″ holes at the ends of the marked slot, and chisel out the remainder to take the musical bank slot. Drill out for belly plug. Sand, and paint. I used blush paint to approximate the generally acknowledged "pink" skin of a pig.

Insert the musical bank slot with a touch of glue on each side. Glue on eyes, and place the plug. The kids are ready to learn to save, to, in this case, "Brahms' Lullaby." ◆

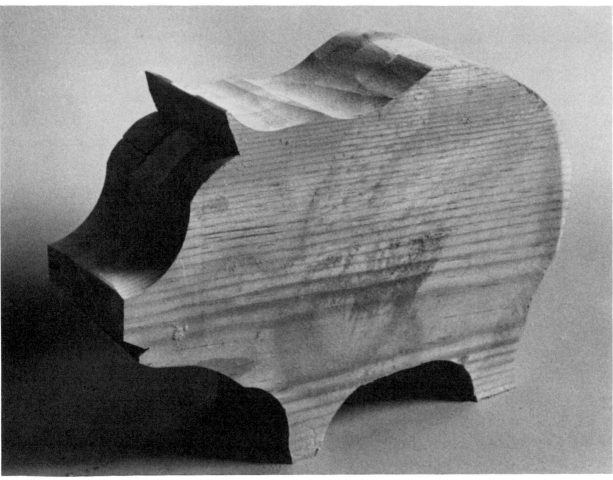

101-1. *Porky in rough outline.*

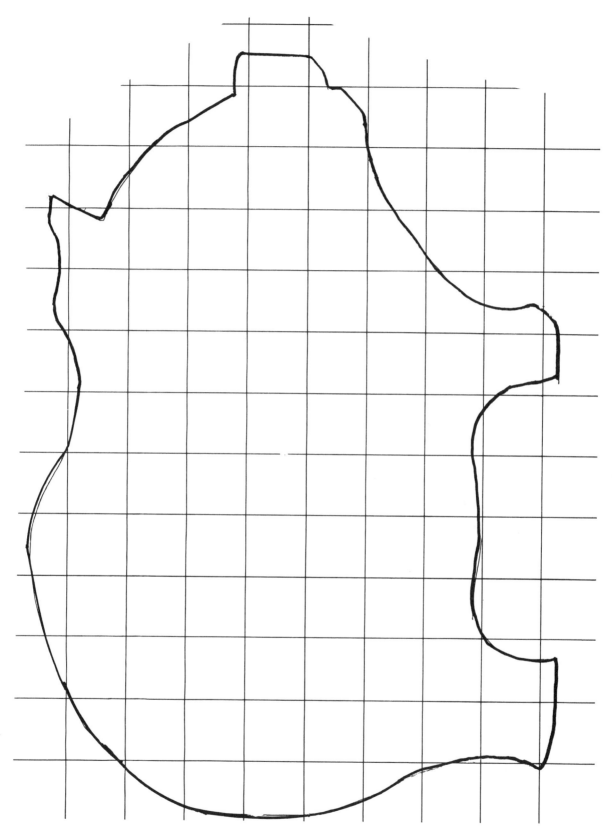

101-2. *Pattern on 1" grid.*

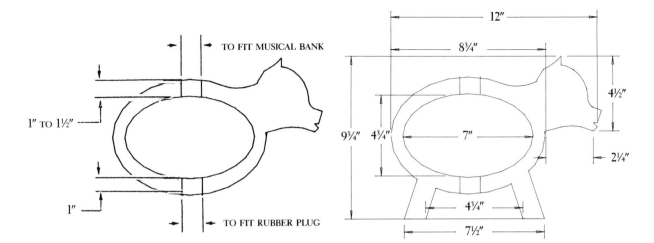

101-3. *Porky bank plan.*

Appendix

Some Useful Woods

Wood	Locale	Characteristics
Ash	East of Rockies in U.S.	Strong, heavy, tough grain that is straight. Sometimes substitutes for more costly oaks.
Basswood	Eastern half of U.S.	Soft, light, weak wood that shrinks considerably. Very uniform, works easily, does not twist or warp.
Beech	East of Mississippi in U.S., southeastern Canada	Similar to birch, shrinks, checks considerably, close grain, may be a light or dark red color.
Birch	East of Mississippi, north of Gulf Coast states in U.S., southeastern Canada, Newfoundland	Hard, durable, fine grain, even texture, heavy and stiff, as well as strong, works easily, takes a high polish. Heartwood is light to dark reddish brown.
Butternut	Southern Canada, Minnesota, eastern U.S., to Alabama, Florida	Much like walnut, but is softer. Not as soft as white pine and basswood, easy to work, fairly strong.
Cherry	Eastern U.S.	Superb-working closed-grained furniture wood. Reddish color, darkens with age if not stained. Durable, strong, easy to machine.
Cypress	Maryland to Texas, U.S.	Resembles white cedar, water-resistant, very durable. May be expensive and difficult to locate.
Douglas fir	Pacific Coast of U.S. and British Columbia in Canada	Strong, light, clear-grained, tends to brittleness. Heartwood somewhat resistant to weathering, available moderately priced, but rising in recent years.
Elm	East of Colorado in U.S.	Slippery, heavy, hard, tough, difficult to split, durable.
Hickory	Arkansas, Tennessee, Ohio, Kentucky in U.S.	Very heavy, hard, tough. Strongest and toughest of our native hardwoods. Checks, shrinks, difficult to work.
Lignum vitae	Central America	Dark greenish-brown wood. Usually hard, closed grained, exceptionally heavy, hard to work, characterized by a soapy feel. Useful for mallets, etc.
Live oak	Coasts of Oregon, California, southern Atlantic and Gulf states in U.S.	Heavy, hard, strong, durable. A bear to work, but superb for small projects otherwise.
Mahogany	Honduras, Mexico, Central America, Florida in U.S., West Indies, Central Africa	Brown to red color, one of the top cabinet woods. Hard, durable, does not split badly, open-grained, but checks, swells, shrinks, warps slightly.
Maple	All U.S. states east of Colorado, southern Canada	Heavy, tough, strong, easy to work, not durable. May be costly. Rock, or sugar, maple is the hardest.

Norway pine	U.S. states along Great Lakes	Light-colored, moderately hard for softwood, not durable, easy to work.
Poplar	Virginia, W. Virginia, Kentucky, along Mississippi Valley in U.S.	Soft, cheap hardwood, good for wide boards—tree grows fast and straight—rots quickly if not protected, works easily. Warps, brittle, fine texture.
Red cedar	East of Colorado, north of Florida in U.S.	Very light, very soft, weak, brittle wood, works easily. May be hard to find in wide boards, very durable.
Red oak	Virginia, W. Virginia, Kentucky, Tennessee, Arkansas, Ohio, Missouri, Maryland, parts of New York in U.S.	Coarse-grained, easily warped and not durable. Forget for outdoor uses.
Redwood	California in U.S.	Ideal construction and durability characteristics. Tends to higher cost, not as strong as yellow pine, but shrinks and splits little, is straight-grained, exceptionally durable with no finish at all. Many inexpensive grades available, and possibly suitable.
Spruce	New York, New England, W. Virginia, Great Lakes states, Idaho, Washington, Oregon in U.S., much of central Canada	Light, soft, fairly durable wood that is close to ideal for outdoor projects.
Sugar pine	California, Oregon in U.S.	Very light, soft, resembles white pine closely.
Walnut	Eastern half of U.S., some in New Mexico, Arizona, California	Fine furniture wood, considered by many to be the ultimate. Coarse-grained, but takes superb finish when pores are filled. Durable, brittle, modest shrinkage, often knotty.
White cedar	Eastern coast of the U.S., around Great Lakes	Soft, light, durable wood, closed-grained, excellent for outdoor uses.
White oak	Virginia, W. Virginia, Tennessee, Arkansas, Ohio, Kentucky, Missouri, Maryland, Indiana in U.S.	Heavy, hard, strong, moderately coarse grain. Tough, dense, most durable of all native American hardwoods, reasonably easy to work (with sharp tools). Tendency to shrink, crack, may be costly in some locales.
White pine	Minnesota, Wisconsin, Maine, Michigan, Idaho, Montana, Oregon, Washington, California, some stands in eastern U.S. other than Maine	Fine-grained, easily worked, sometimes found with few knots. Durable, soft, not exceptionally strong, economical, excellent for many uses. White in color, shrinks, does not split easily.
Yellow pine	Virginia to Texas in U.S., some species classed as southern pine	Hard, tough softwood. Heartwood is fairly durable, hard to nail, saws and generally works easily, inexpensive, excellent for outdoor uses. Grain variable, reddish brown in color, heavy for a softwood, resinous.

Softwood Lumber Grades

Product	Grade	Character
Adapted from chart by the Southern Forest Products Association		
Finish	B&B	Highest grade, generally clear, limited number of pin knots allowed. Natural or stain finish.
	C	Excellent for paint, or natural with lower needs. Limited number surface checks and small, tight knots allowed.
	C&Btr	Combination of above two grades.
	D	Economical, serviceable for natural or painted finish.
Boards S4S	1	High quality, good appearance. Sound and tight-knotted, largest hole permitted $\frac{1}{16}''$. Forms, shelving, crating.
	2	High-quality sheathing. Tight knots, mostly free of holes.
	3	Good, serviceable sheathing.
	4	Pieces like No. 3, but below, with usable lengths at least 24''. A useful grade for many projects.
Dimension structural light framing 2''–4'' thick 2''–4'' wide	Select structural, Dense select structural	High quality, reasonably free of strength defects.
	1 & 1 Dense	Hight strength, general use, good appearance, limited knots.
	2 & 2 Dense	Not as good as No. 1, still for all construction. Tight knots.
	3 & 3 Dense	High quality, low cost, appearance not as good as No. 2, may be limited by single factor.
Studs 2''–4'' thick 2''–6'' wide 10' or shorter	Stud	Stringent requirements as to straightness, strength, stiffness, for all stud uses, including load-bearing walls. Good for a lot of pet housing purposes.
Light framing 2''–4'' thick 2''–4'' wide	Construction	For general framing purposes. Appearance is good, strong, serviceable.
	Standard	Same uses as above, but allows larger defects.
	Utility	For blocking, plate, braces.
	Economy	Similar to Utility, but with shorter usable lengths, best used where strength, appearance are not critical.

Softwood Plywood Grades

Softwood plywood grading standards, for members of the American Plywood Association, start with face grades which vary from A down to C.

A is a sanded face, for painting or staining, of A-A grade, in interior or exterior plywood, made with minimum D interior filler plies (interior) and C (exterior), for uses where both faces show. A-B has a second face not as good as the A face, but suitable for painting. With A-C only exterior type is made. A-D is only in interior grade.

B grades work down, with a less pretty face ply. B grades are for surfaces that will be painted or covered with other materials (such as laminates, veneers, etc.).

C grades are often unsanded, and have open spots in the face (C-C Plugged has most of those filled). C-C is lowest of exterior plywood grades, for rough work such as sheathing. C-D is interior rough construction type, made with exterior glues. Called CDX, it is not for permanent outdoor use.

Oriented strand board (OSB) is wood panelling of aligned wood strands bonded, with resins, under heat and pressure. Strands are in layers, at right angles to each other. **Waferboard** is similar, made from wood wafers.

Veneer grade N is natural-finish veneer, and may be all heartwood or all sapwood. Repairs must be parallel to the

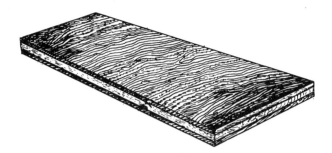

Plywood. Three plies are common for ⅛″ and ¼″ plywood. Thicker varieties may have as many as 15 plies—but always an odd number.

grain, matched for grain and color. This is the most costly softwood plywood.

Softwood plywood isn't pretty when stained, so a painted finish is best. If a natural finish is needed, lower-grade solid pine is no more expensive than pine plywood.

Plywood is laid up in odd-numbered piles, with ⅛″ and ¼″ panels having three plies, ⅜″ and ½″ thicknesses with five plies, and so on. Sheets are available in 4′ widths and lengths from 8′ to 12′.

Metric Conversion

Inches to Millimetres and Centimetres							
	MM—millimetres			*CM—centimetres*			
Inches	**MM**	**CM**	**Inches**	**CM**	**Inches**	**CM**	
⅛	3	0.3	9	22.9	30	76.2	
¼	6	0.6	10	25.4	31	78.7	
⅜	10	1.0	11	27.9	32	81.3	
½	13	1.3	12	30.5	33	83.8	
⅝	16	1.6	13	33.0	34	86.4	
¾	19	1.9	14	35.6	35	88.9	
⅞	22	2.2	15	38.1	36	91.4	
1	25	2.5	16	40.6	37	94.0	
1¼	32	3.2	17	43.2	38	96.5	
1½	38	3.8	18	45.7	39	99.1	
1¾	44	4.4	19	48.3	40	101.6	
2	51	5.1	20	50.8	41	104.1	
2½	64	6.4	21	53.3	42	106.7	
3	76	7.6	22	55.9	43	109.2	
3½	89	8.9	23	58.4	44	111.8	
4	102	10.2	24	61.0	45	114.3	
4½	114	11.4	25	63.5	46	116.8	
5	127	12.7	26	66.0	47	119.4	
6	152	15.2	27	68.6	48	121.9	
7	178	17.8	28	71.1	49	124.5	
8	203	20.3	29	73.7	50	127.0	

Index